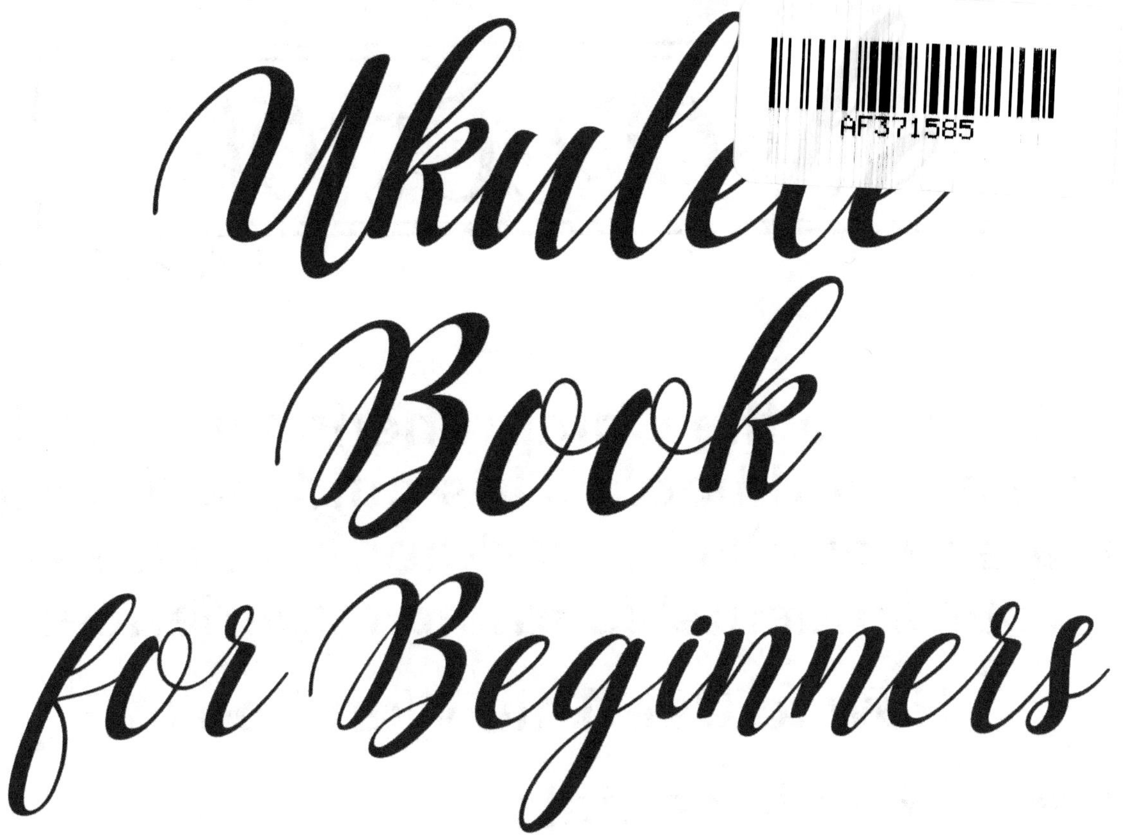

Ukulele Book for Beginners

____

____

Welcome to the Comprehensive Ukulele Strumming Workbook! This guide will help you navigate through the workbook and maximize your students' learning experience.

How to Use This Workbook

1.Start with Fundamentals:

- Begin with the Rhythm Notation and Time Signatures sections to build a solid foundation.

- Familiarize students with Strumming Symbols and Counting Rhythms.

2.Engage with Activities:

- Use the Writing Up & Down Strum Symbols and Rhythm Counting exercises to reinforce concepts.

- Progress to Rhythm & Strumming Exercises for practical application.

- Encourage creativity with Rhythm Compositions and Strum Pattern Compositions.

3.Cover All Combinations:

- Ensure students practice all rhythm combinations to achieve mastery.

- The workbook includes exercises in 4/4, 3/4, and 2/4 time signatures, covering quarter, eighth, and sixteenth notes, as well as quarter rests.

4.Customize and Assess:

- Use the Teacher Editable Versions to tailor activities to your students' needs.

- Include empty chord charts in activities for customized strumming practice.

5.Tips for Success

- Consistent Practice: Encourage daily practice to reinforce new skills.

- Interactive Learning: Make use of group activities and peer feedback.

- Track Progress: Regularly assess students to monitor improvement and adjust the difficulty level accordingly.

This workbook is designed to make learning rhythm and strumming both accessible and enjoyable. Happy teaching!

Rhythm Counting Studies

Write above the rhythms which beat they are on. (1 & 2 & 3 & 4 &)

1.

2.

3.

4.

Rhythm Counting Studies

Write which beat each rhythm is on the space above. (1 e & a 2 e & a 3 e & a 4 e & a)

1.

2.

3.

4.

Strumming Exercises
Strum the rhythms below.

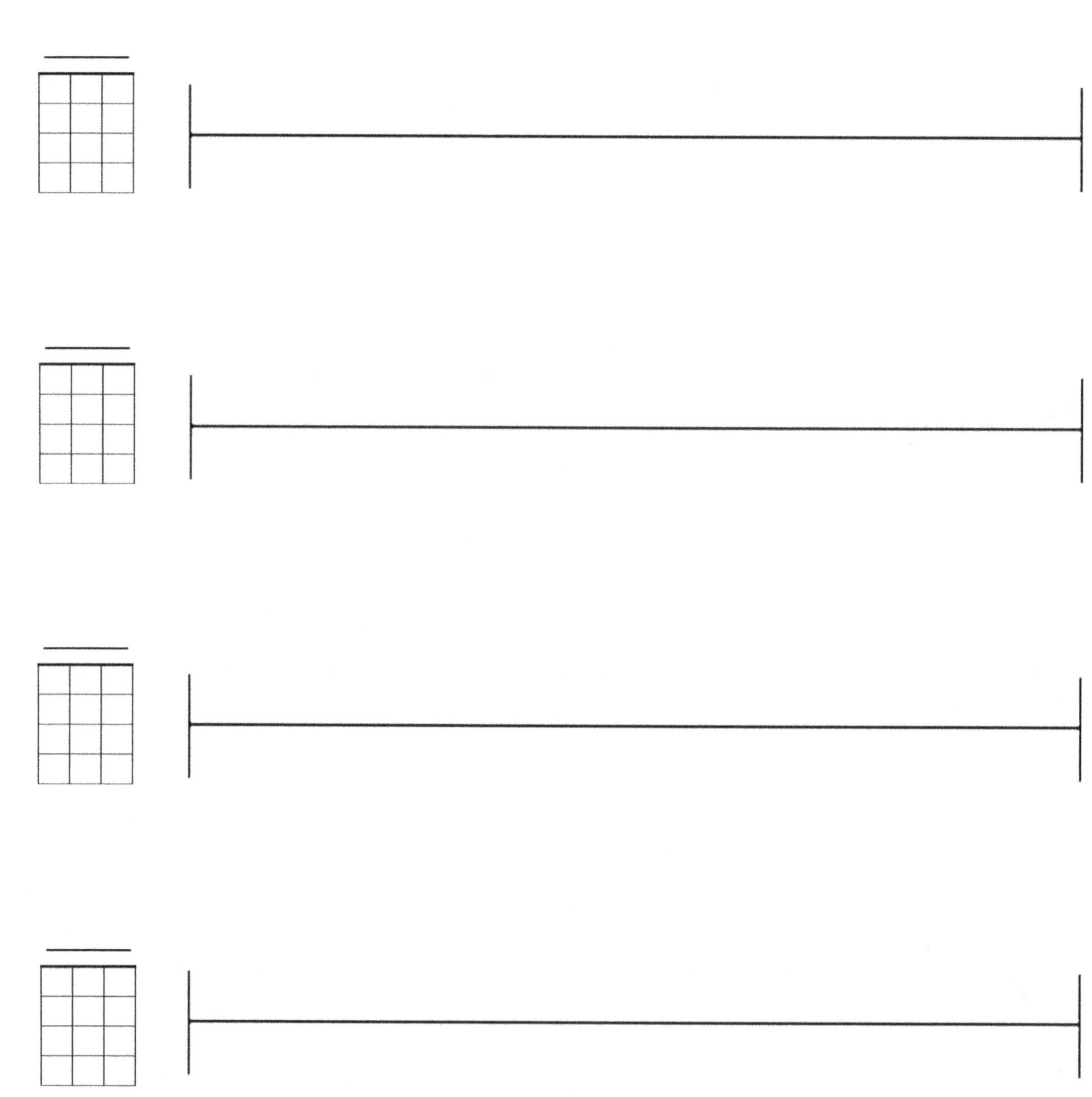

Strumming Studies

Write the strum pattern symbols above
each of the rhythms below.

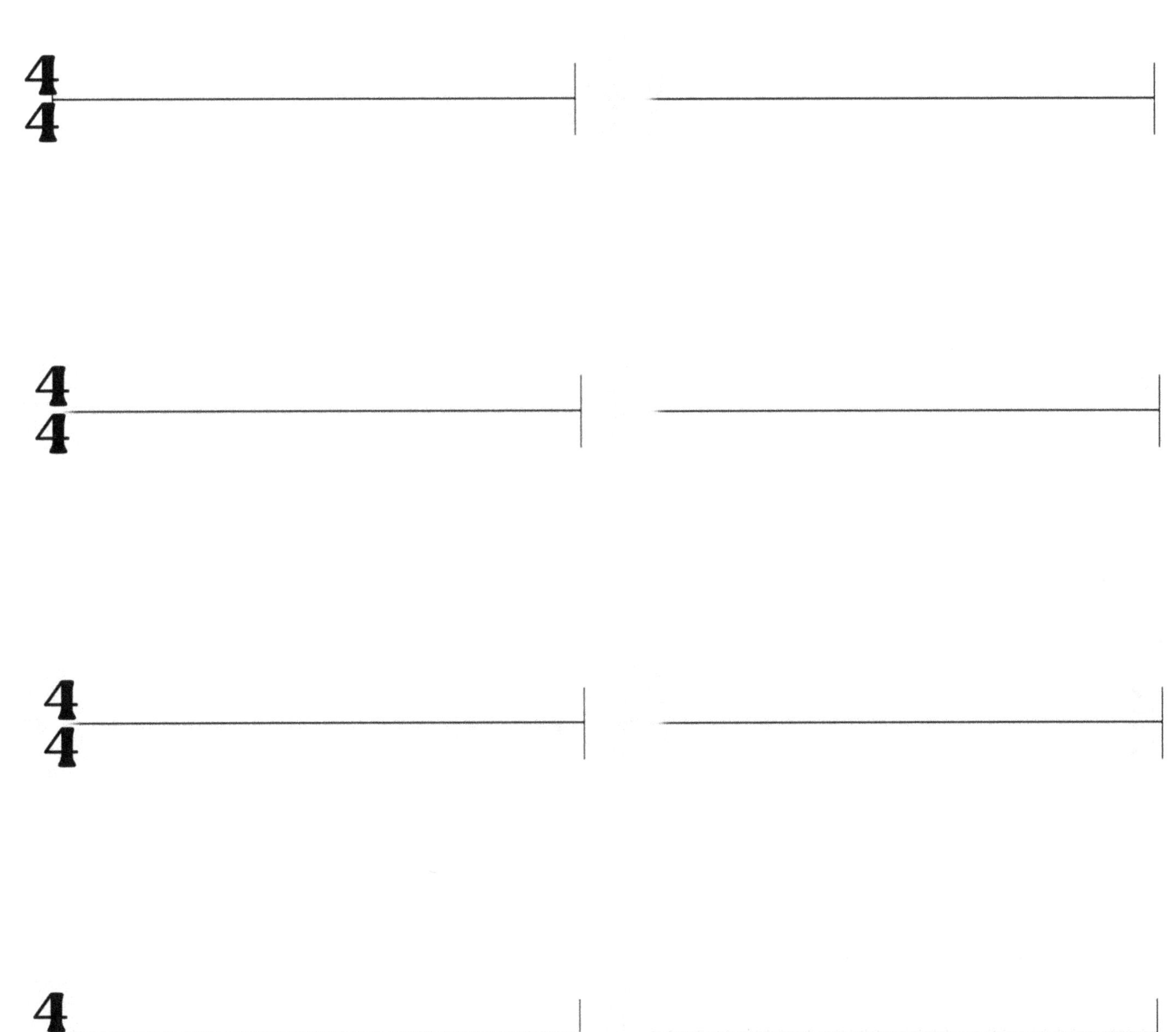

Strumming Studies

Write the strum pattern symbols above
each of the rhythms below.

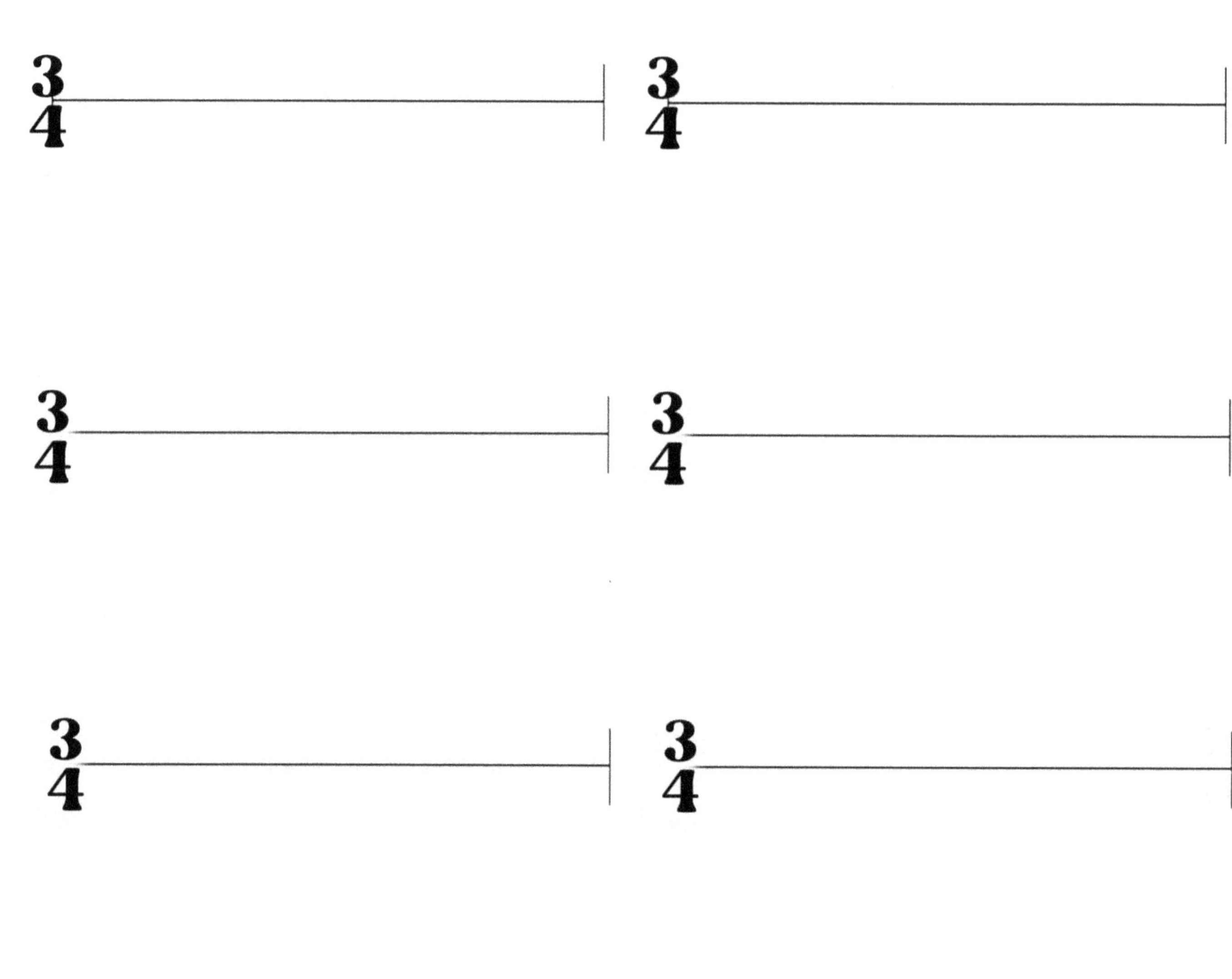

Strumming Studies

Write the strum pattern symbols above
each of the rhythms below.

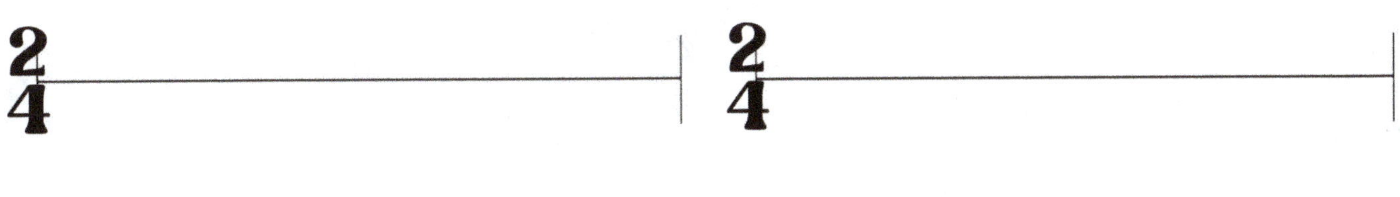

Rhythm Counting Studies

Write which beat each rhythm is on the space above. (1 & 2 & 3 & 4 &)

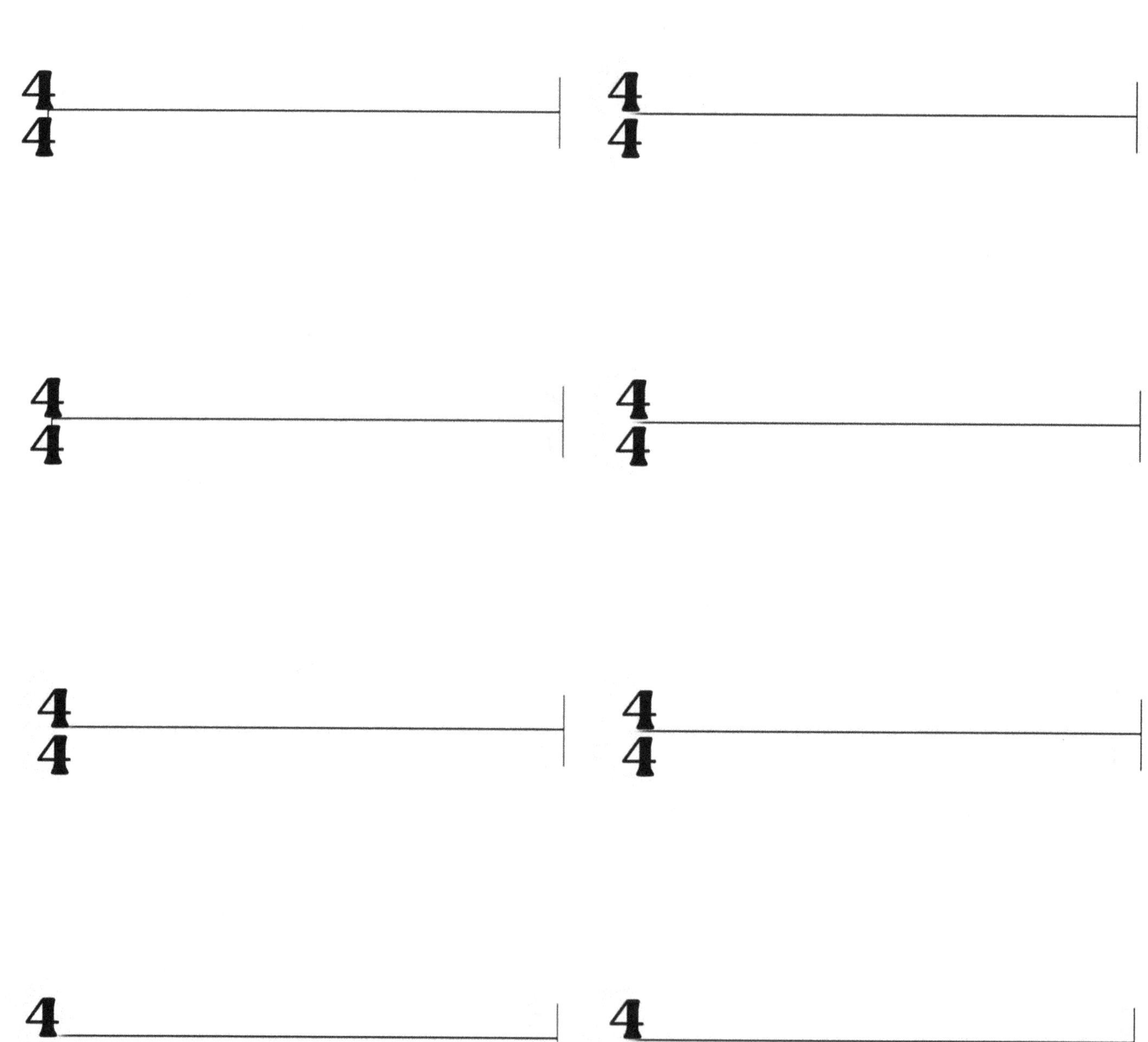

Rhythm Counting Studies

Write which beat each rhythm is on the space above. (1 & 2 & 3 & 4 &)

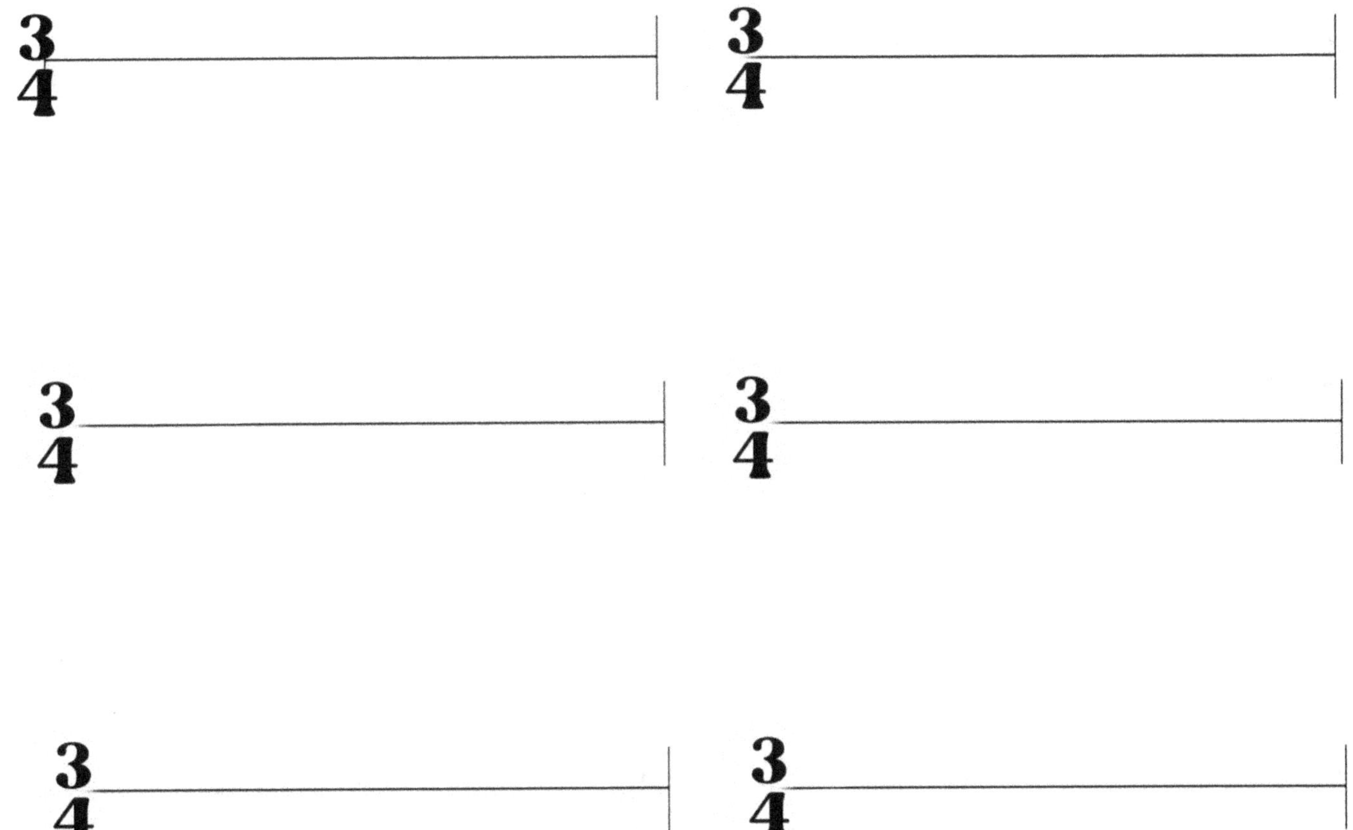

Rhythm Counting Studies

Write which beat each rhythm is on the space above. (1 & 2 & 3 & 4)

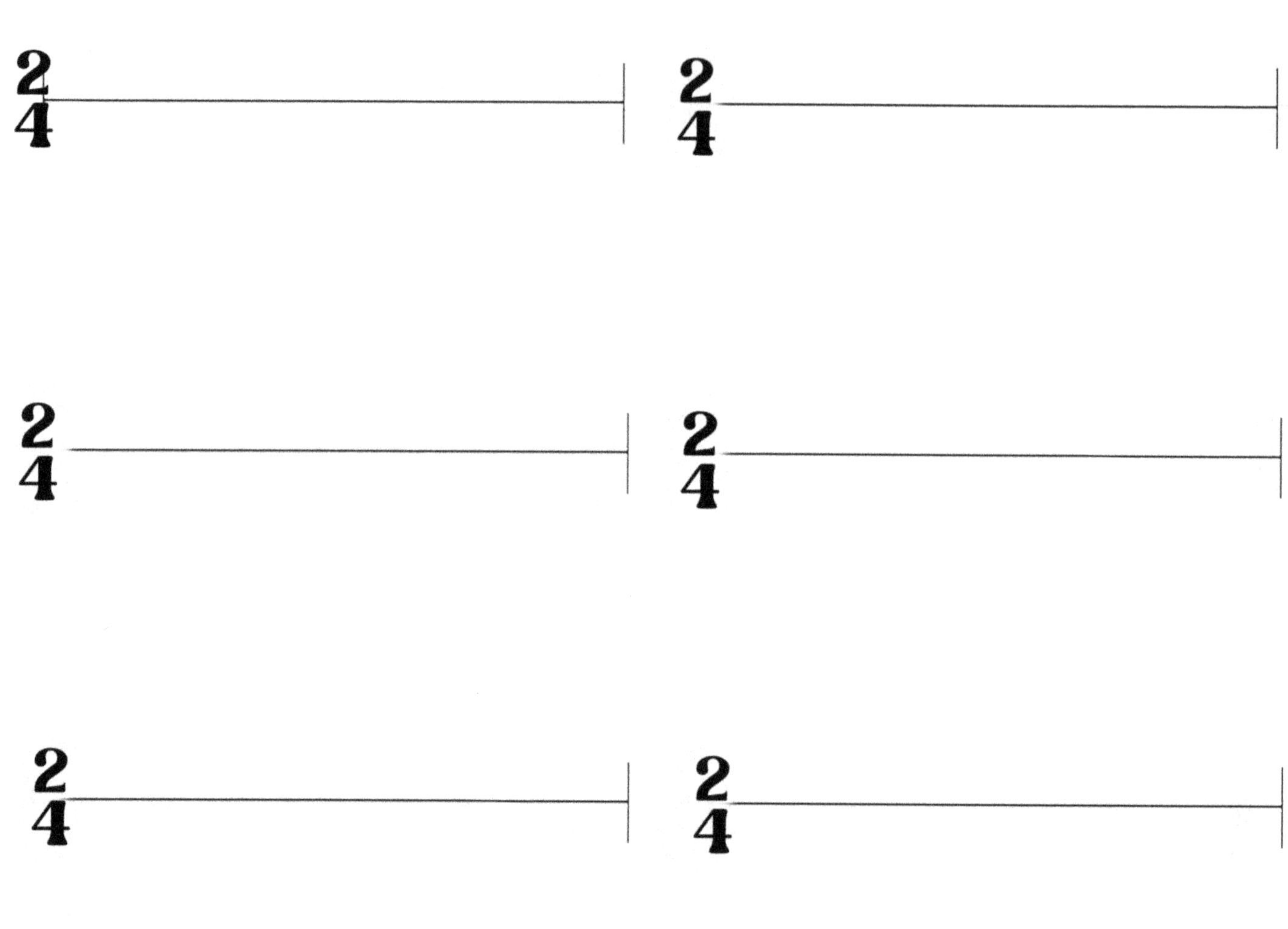

Rhythm Counting Studies

Write which beat each rhythm is on the space above. (1 e & a 2 e & a 3 e & a 4 e & a)

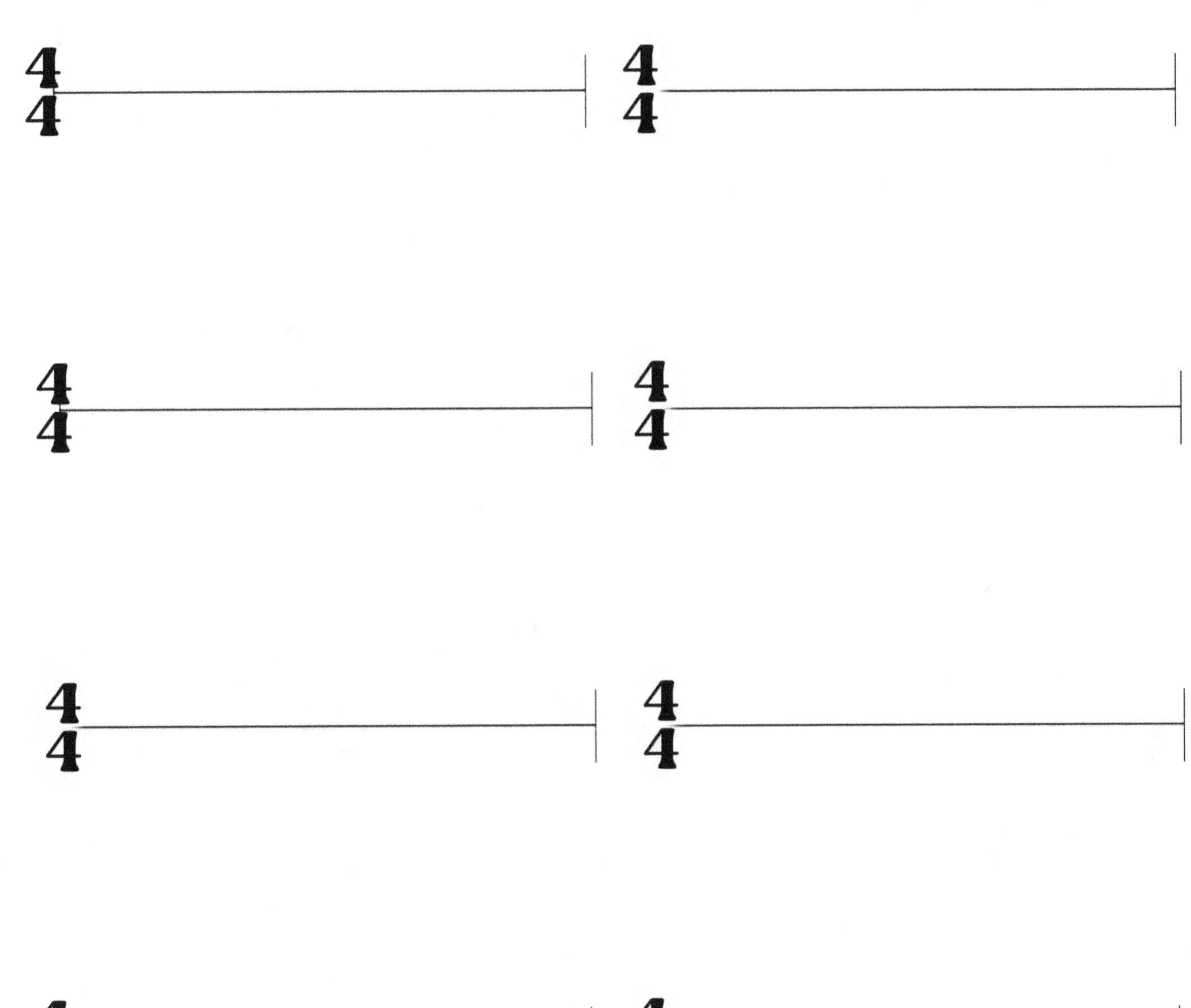

Rhythm Counting Studies

Write which beat each rhythm is on the space above. (1 e & a 2 e & a 3 e & a 4 e & a)

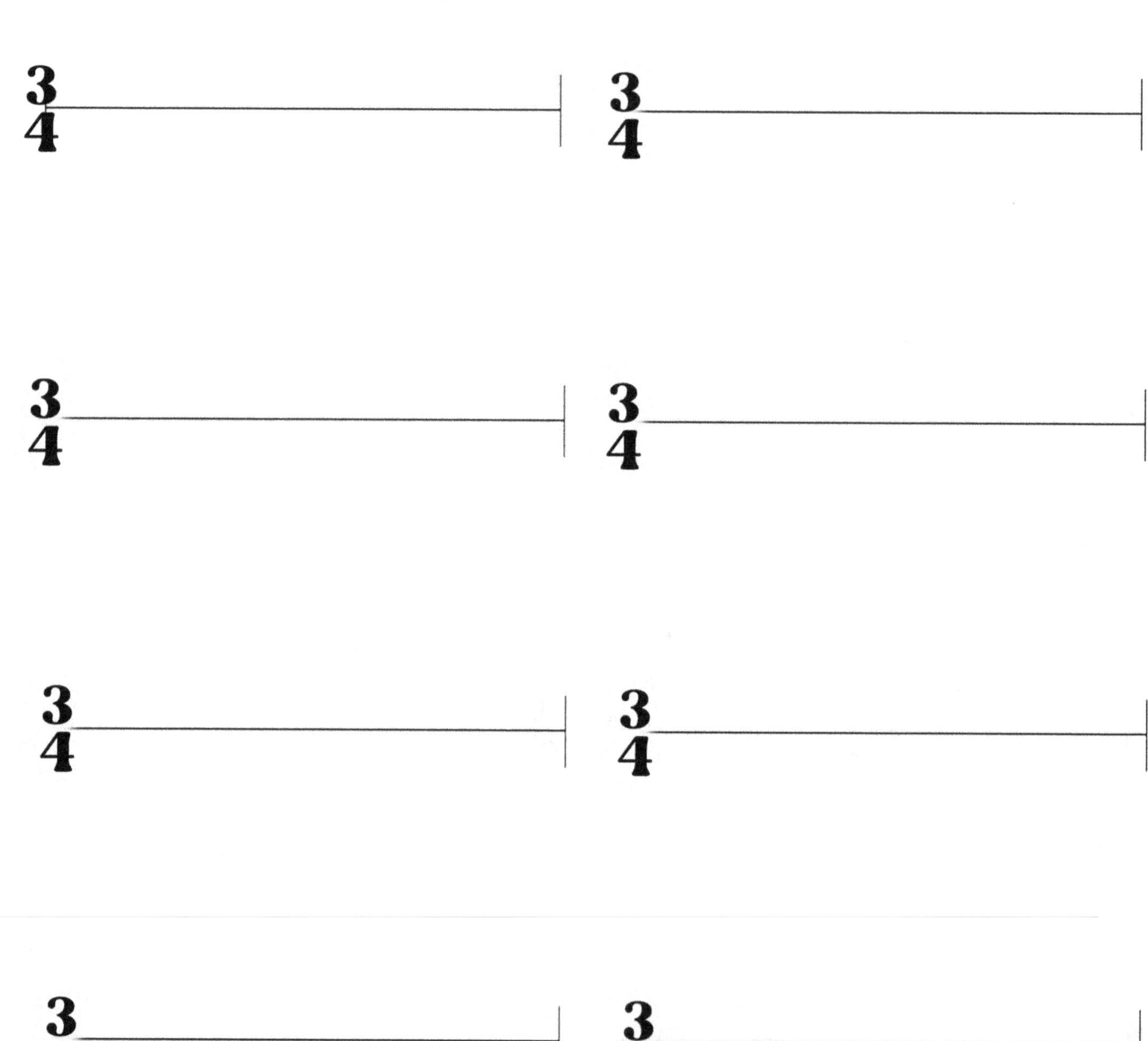

Rhythm Counting Studies

Write which beat each rhythm is on the space above. (1 e & a 2 e & a 3 e & a)

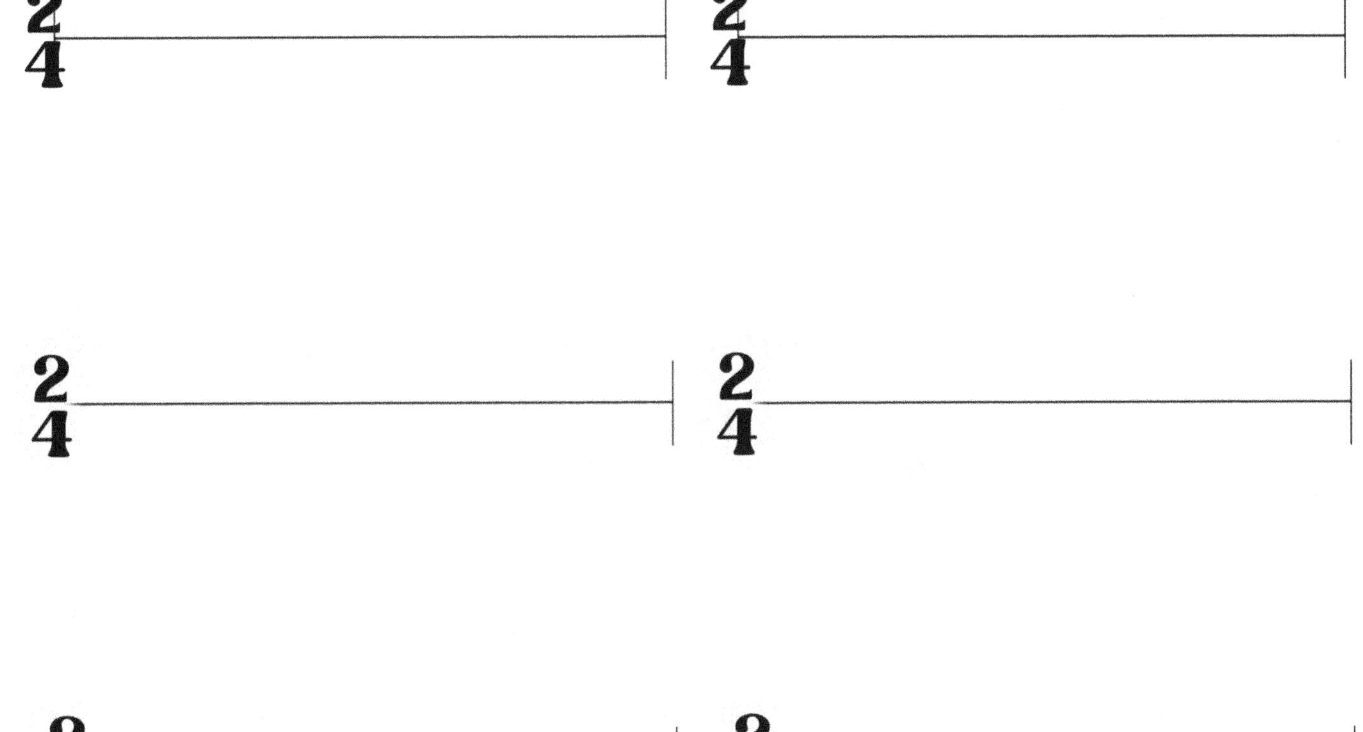

Strumming Exercises

Strum the rhythms below.

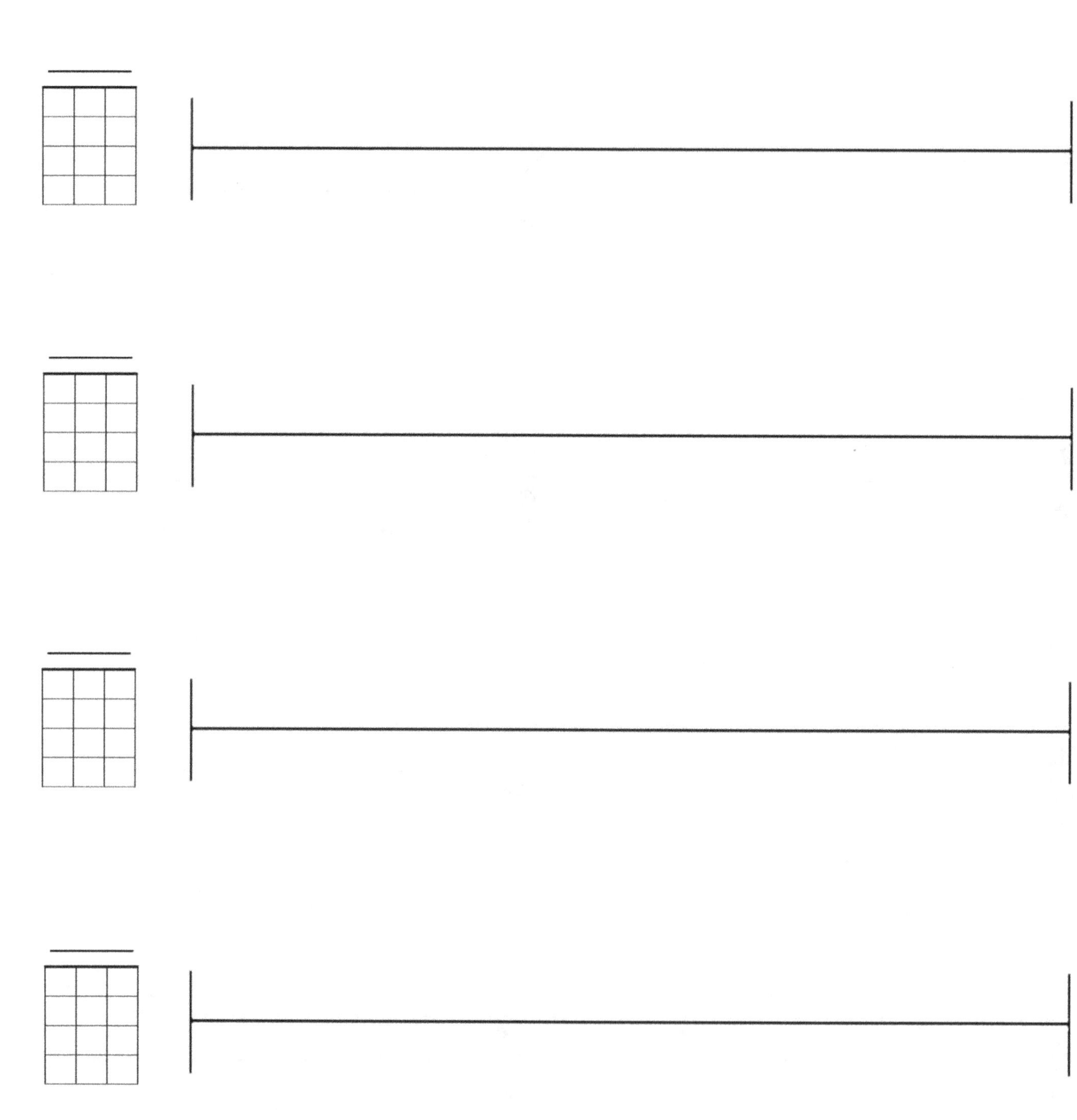

Strumming Studies

Write the strum pattern symbols above each of the rhythms below.

Strumming Studies

Write the strum pattern symbols above
each of the rhythms below.

Strumming Studies

Write the strum pattern symbols above
each of the rhythms below.

Strumming Studies

Write the strum pattern symbols above
each of the rhythms below.

Strumming Studies

Write the strum pattern symbols above each of the rhythms below.

Strumming Studies

Write the strum pattern symbols above each of the rhythms below.

Strumming Studies

Write the strum pattern symbols above each of the rhythms below.

Strumming Studies

Write the strum pattern symbols above each of the rhythms below.

Strumming Studies

Write the strum pattern symbols above each of the rhythms below.

Strumming Studies

Write the strum pattern symbols above each of the rhythms below.

Rhythm Counting Studies

Write which beat each rhythm is on the space above. (1 & 2 & 3 & 4 &)

Rhythm Counting Studies

Write which beat each rhythm is on the space above. (1 & 2 & 3 & 4 &)

Rhythm Counting Studies

Write which beat each rhythm is on the space above. (1 & 2 & 3 & 4 &)

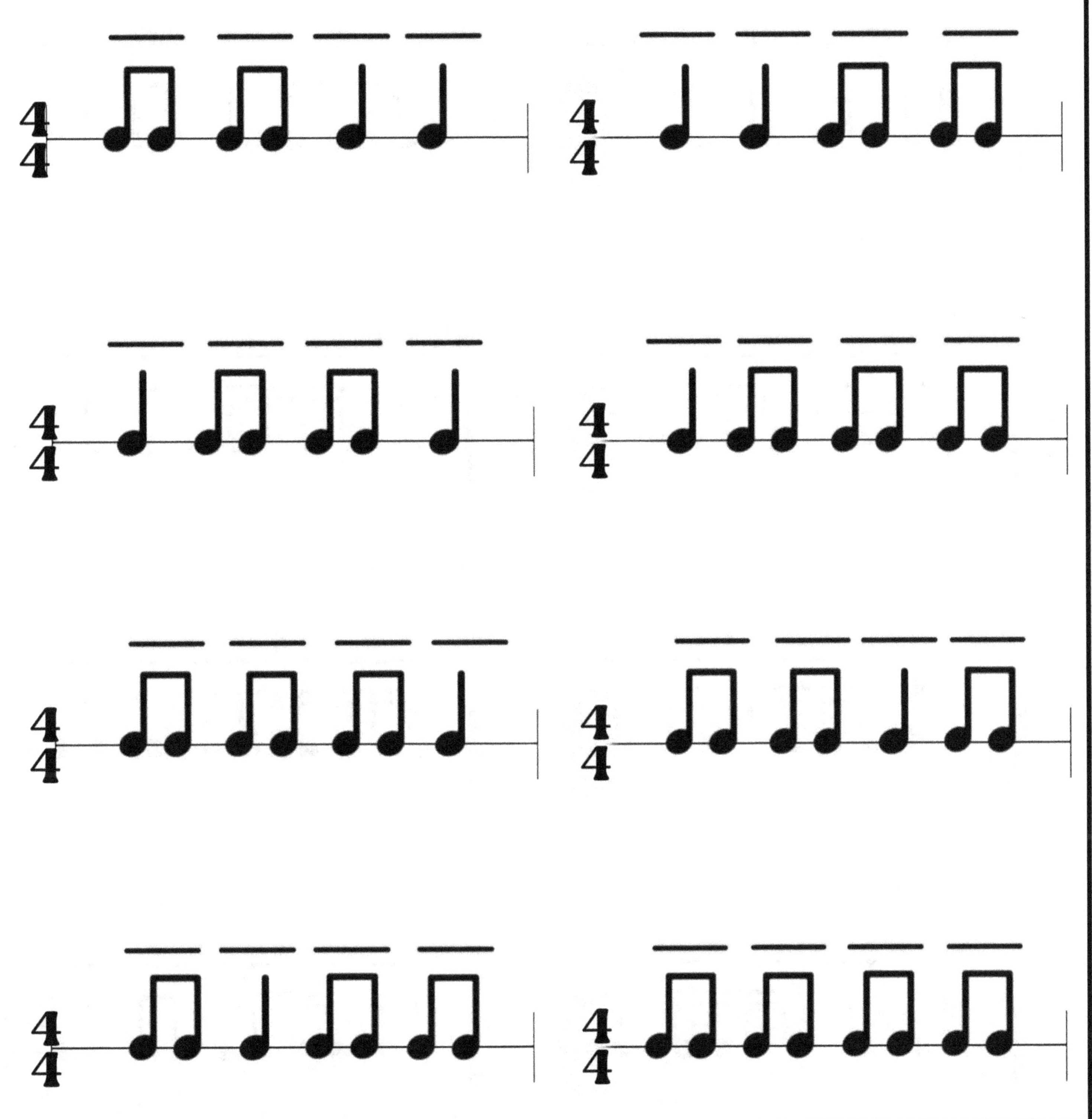

Rhythm Counting Studies

Write which beat each rhythm is on the space above. (1 e & a 2 e & a 3 e & a 4 e & a)

Rhythm Counting Studies

Write which beat each rhythm is on the space above. (1 & 2 & 3 & 4 &)

Rhythm Counting Studies

Write which beat each rhythm is on the space above. (1 & 2 & 3 & 4 &)

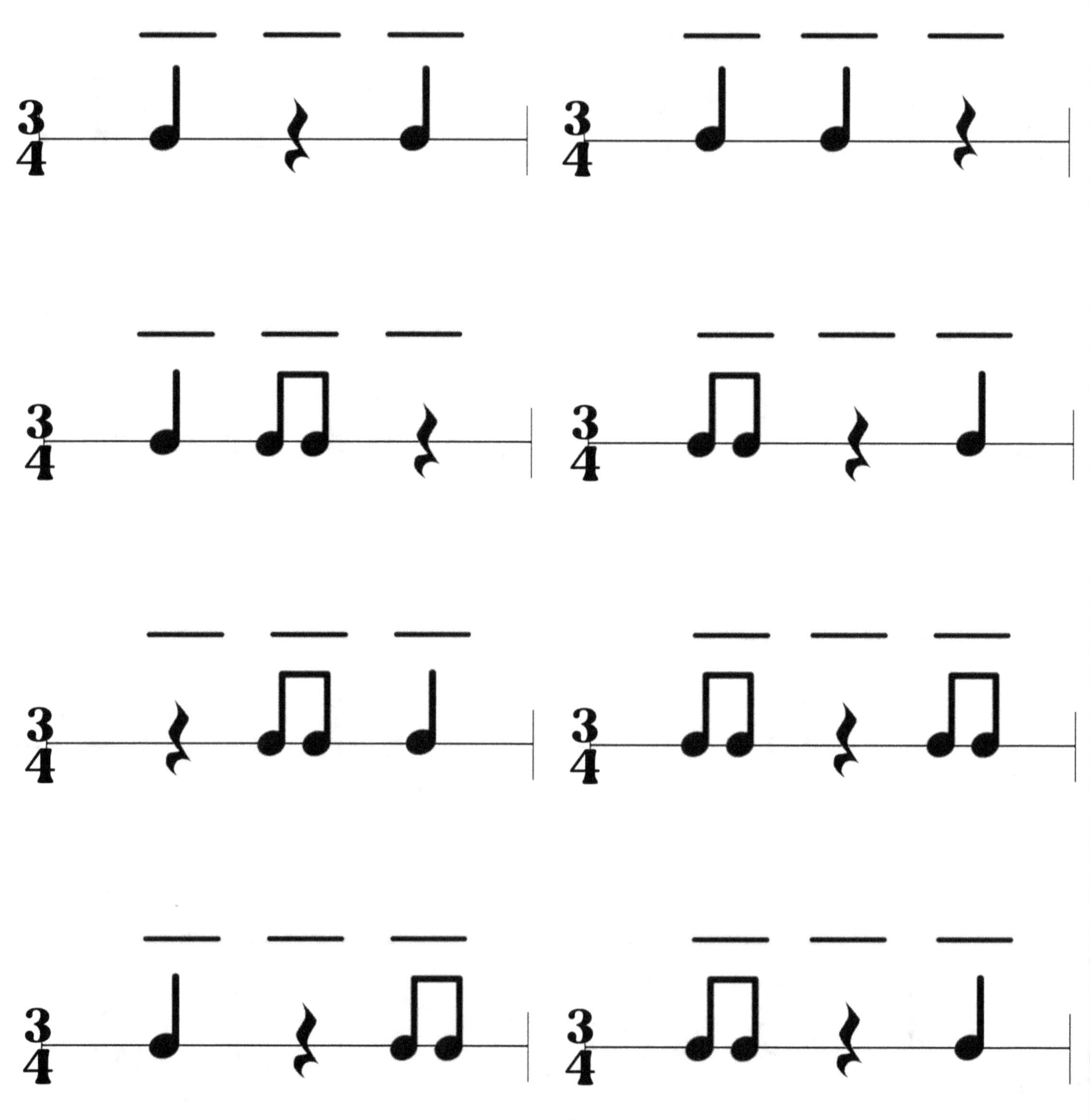

Rhythm Counting Studies

Write which beat each rhythm is on the space above. (1 & 2 & 3 & 4 &)

Rhythm Counting Studies

Write which beat each rhythm is on the space above. (1 e & a 2 e & a 3 e & a 4 e & a)

Strumming Studies

Strum the rhythms below.

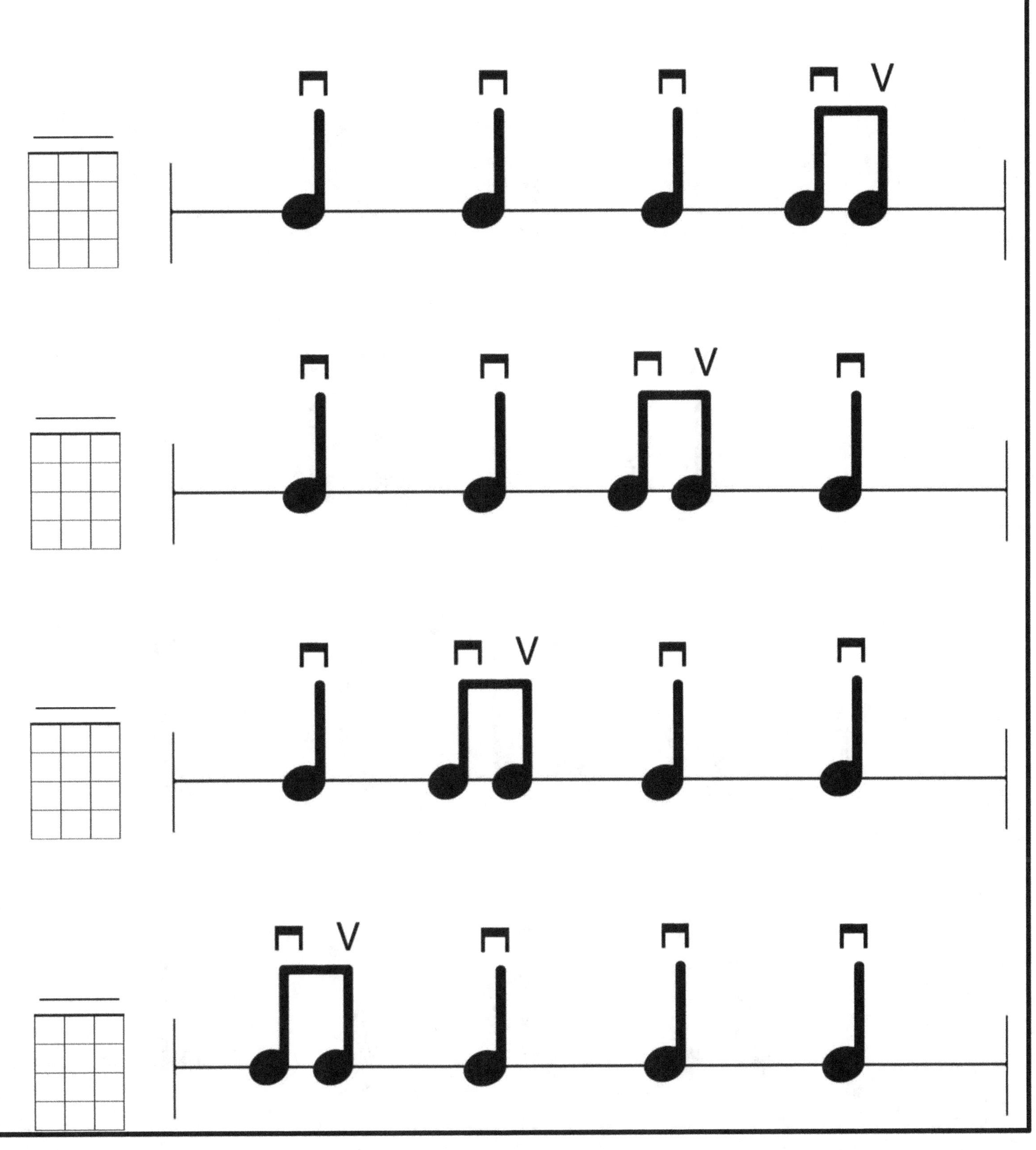

Strumming Exercises
Strum the rhythms below.

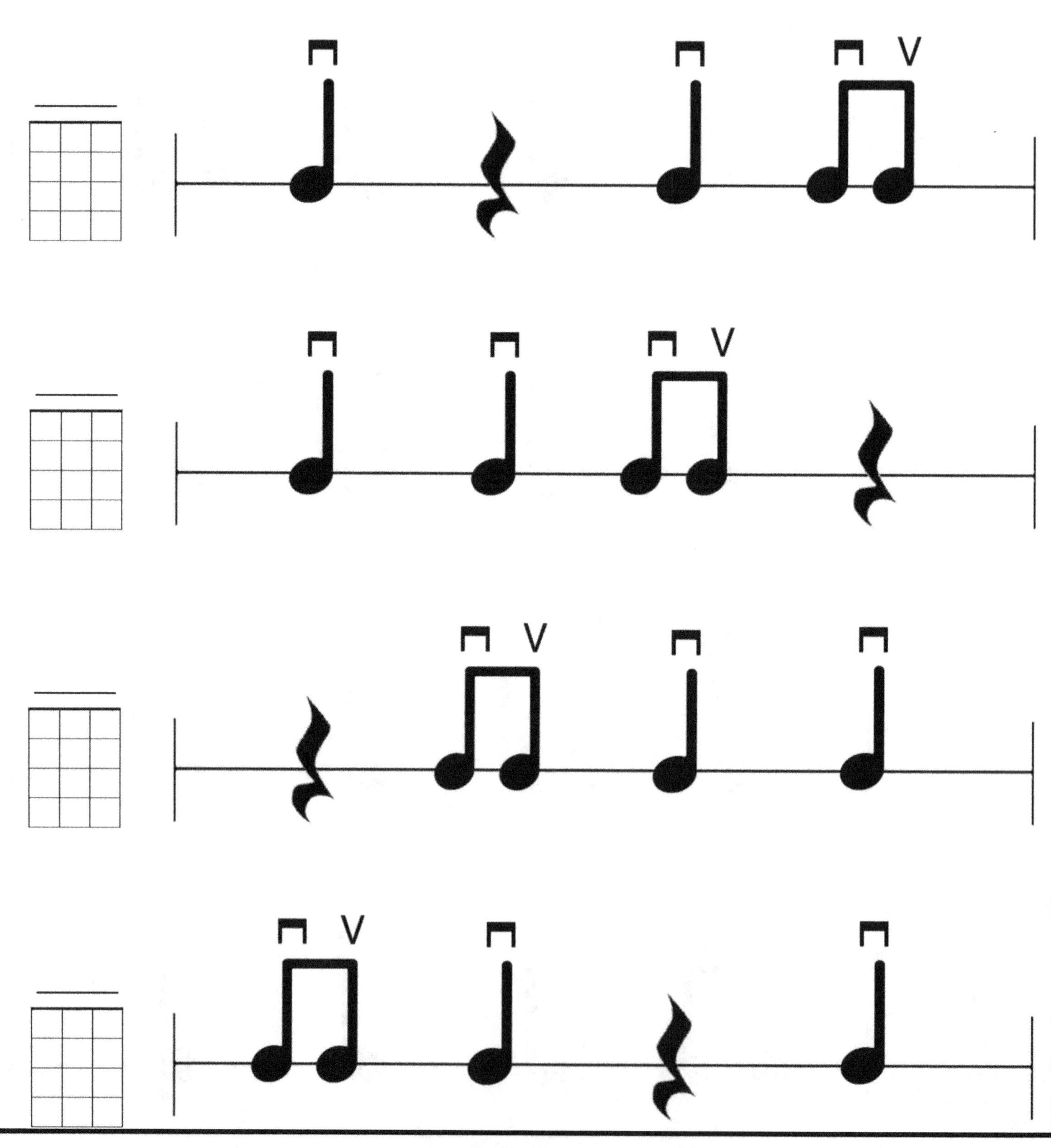

Strumming Exercises
Strum the rhythms below.

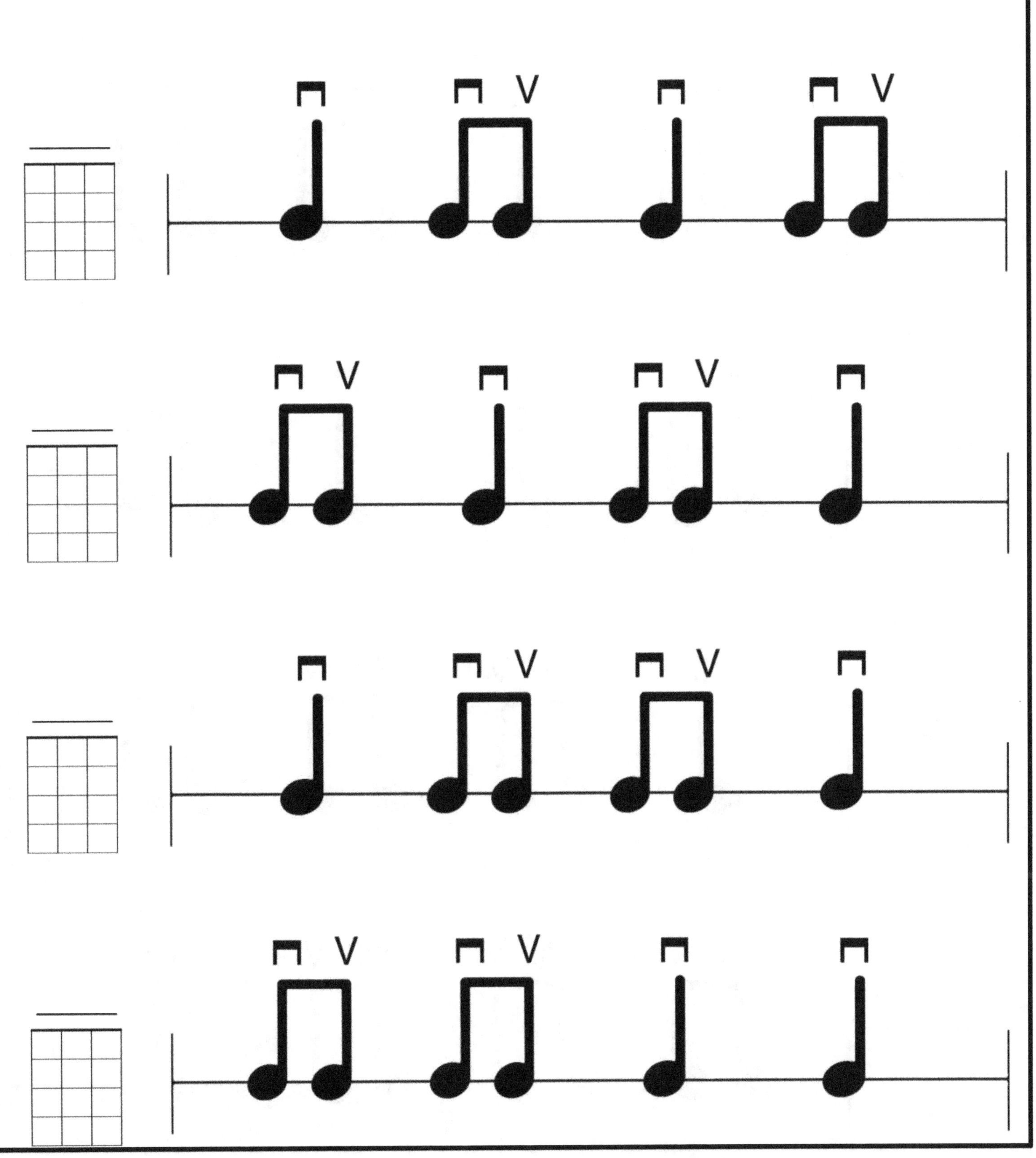

Strumming Exercises

Strum the rhythms below.

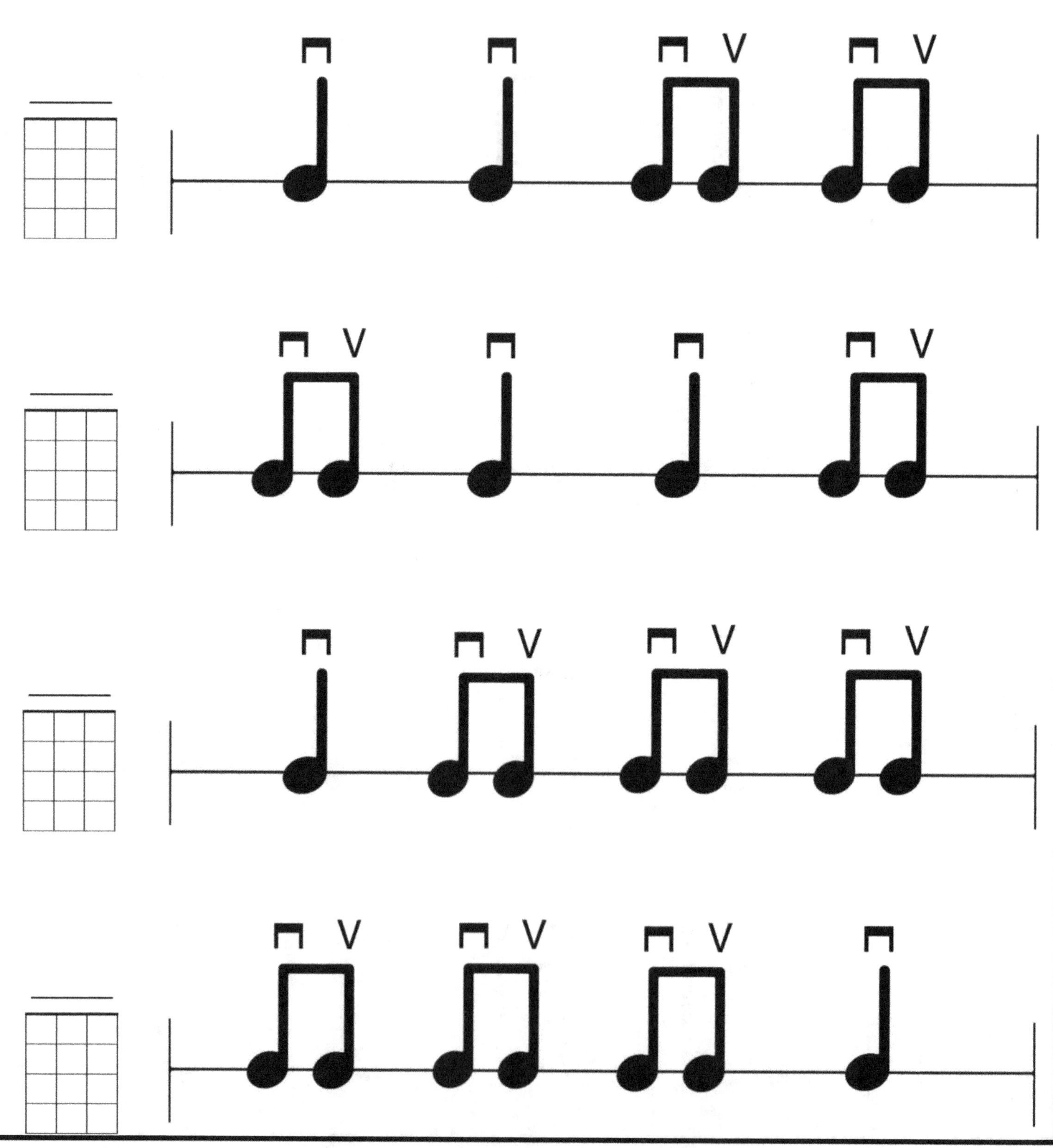

Strumming Exercises
Strum the rhythms below.

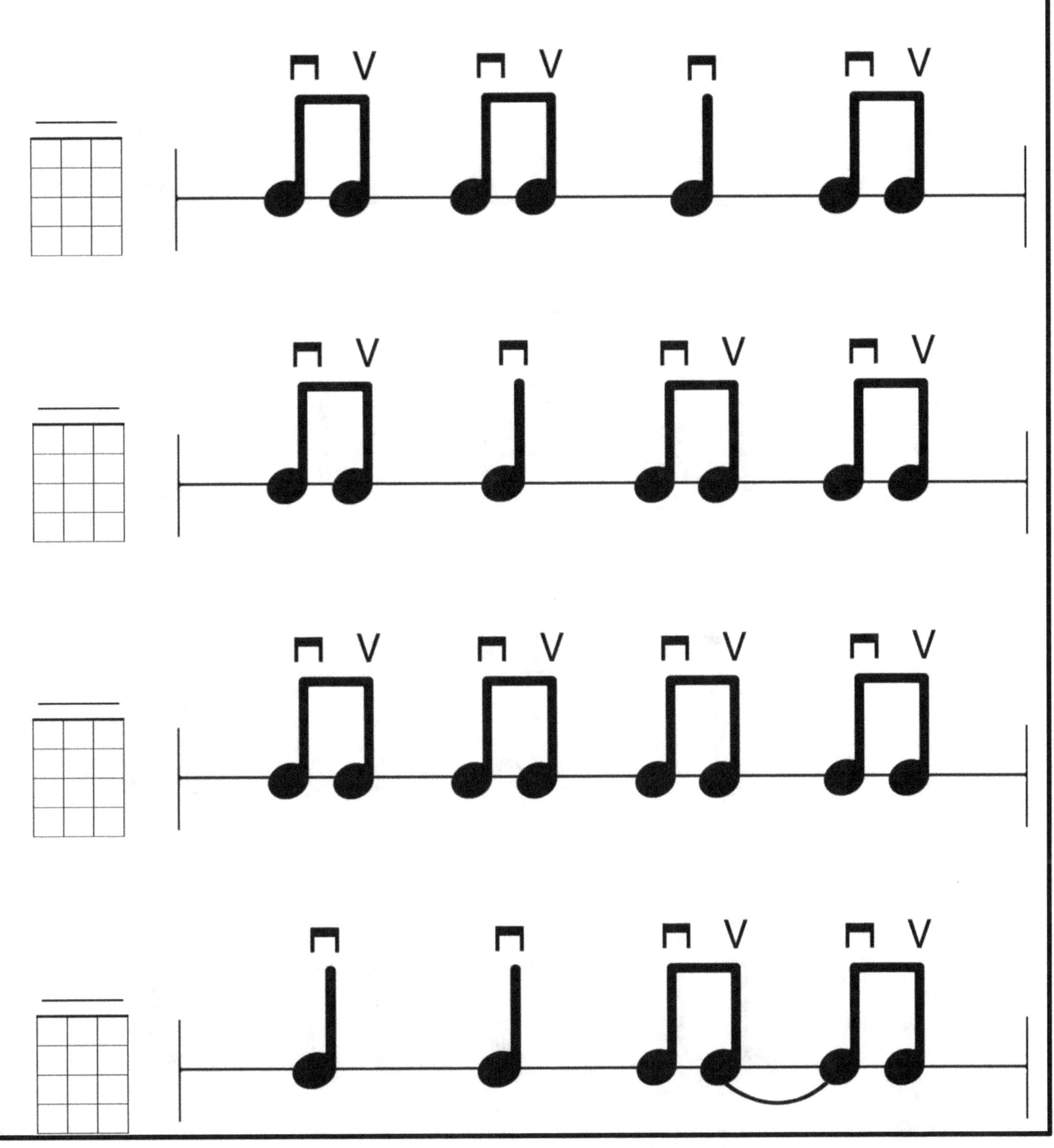

Strumming Exercises
Strum the rhythms below.

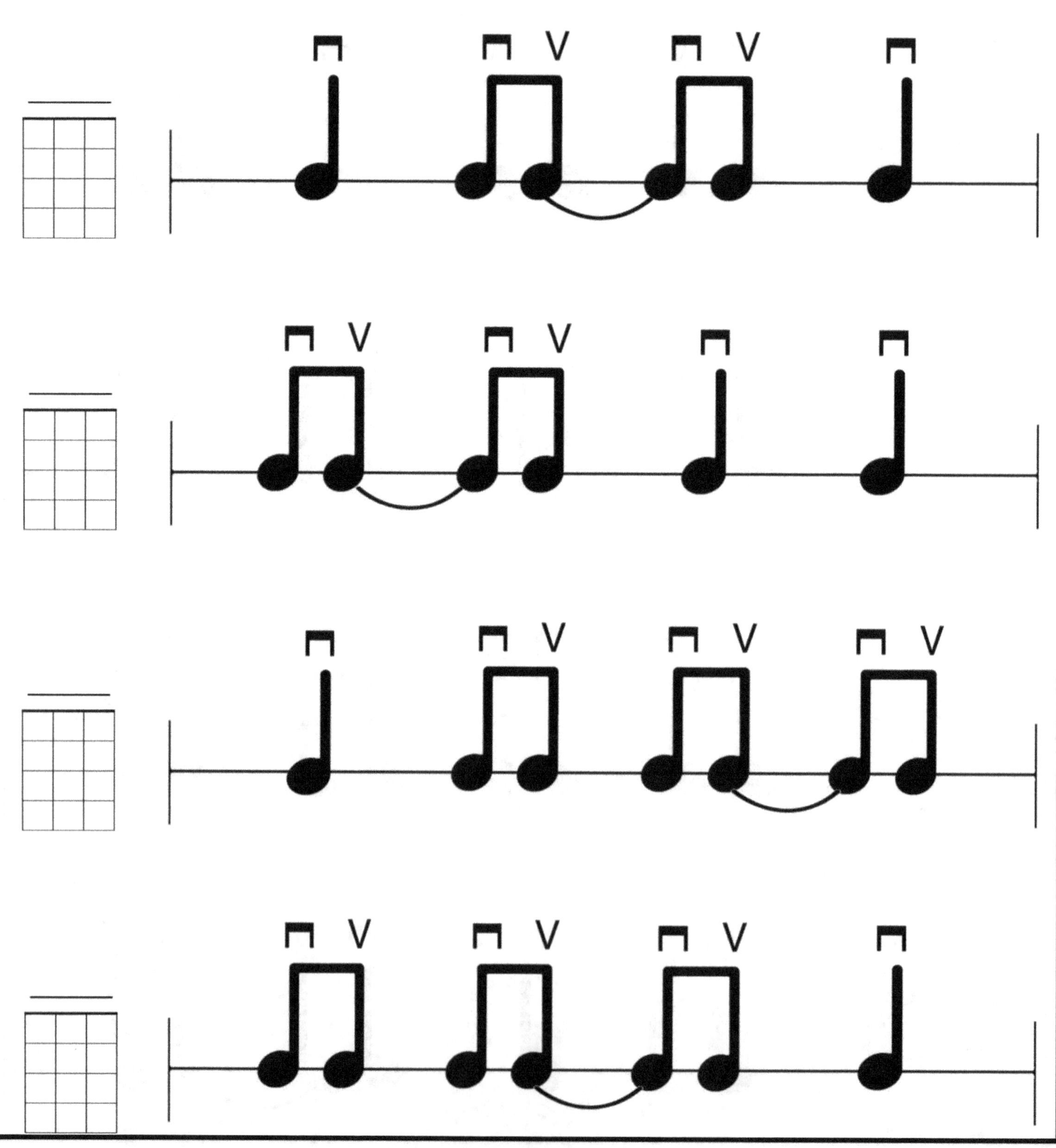

Strumming Exercises

Strum the rhythms below.

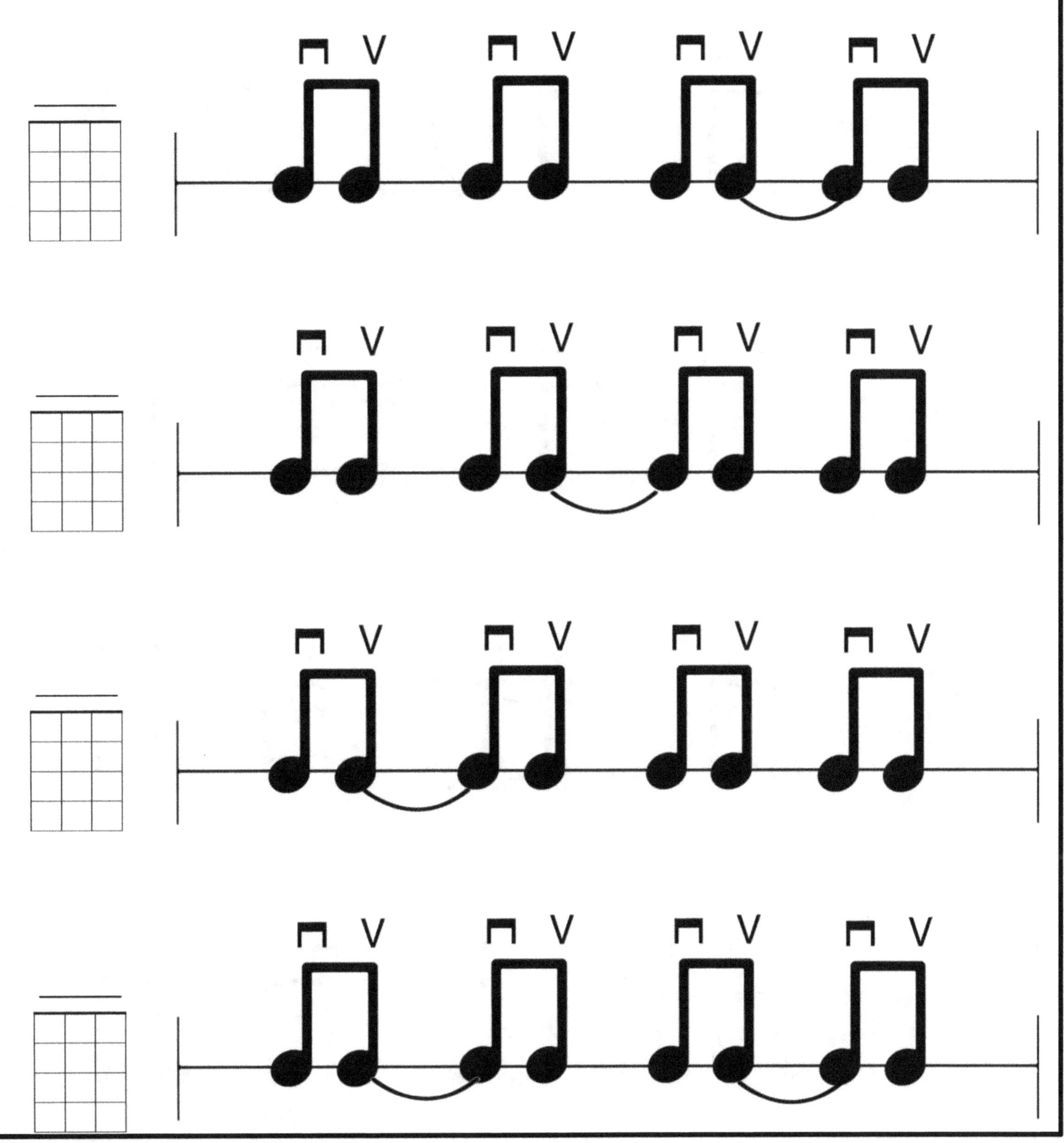

Strumming Exercises
Strum the rhythms below.

Strumming Exercises

Strum the rhythms below.

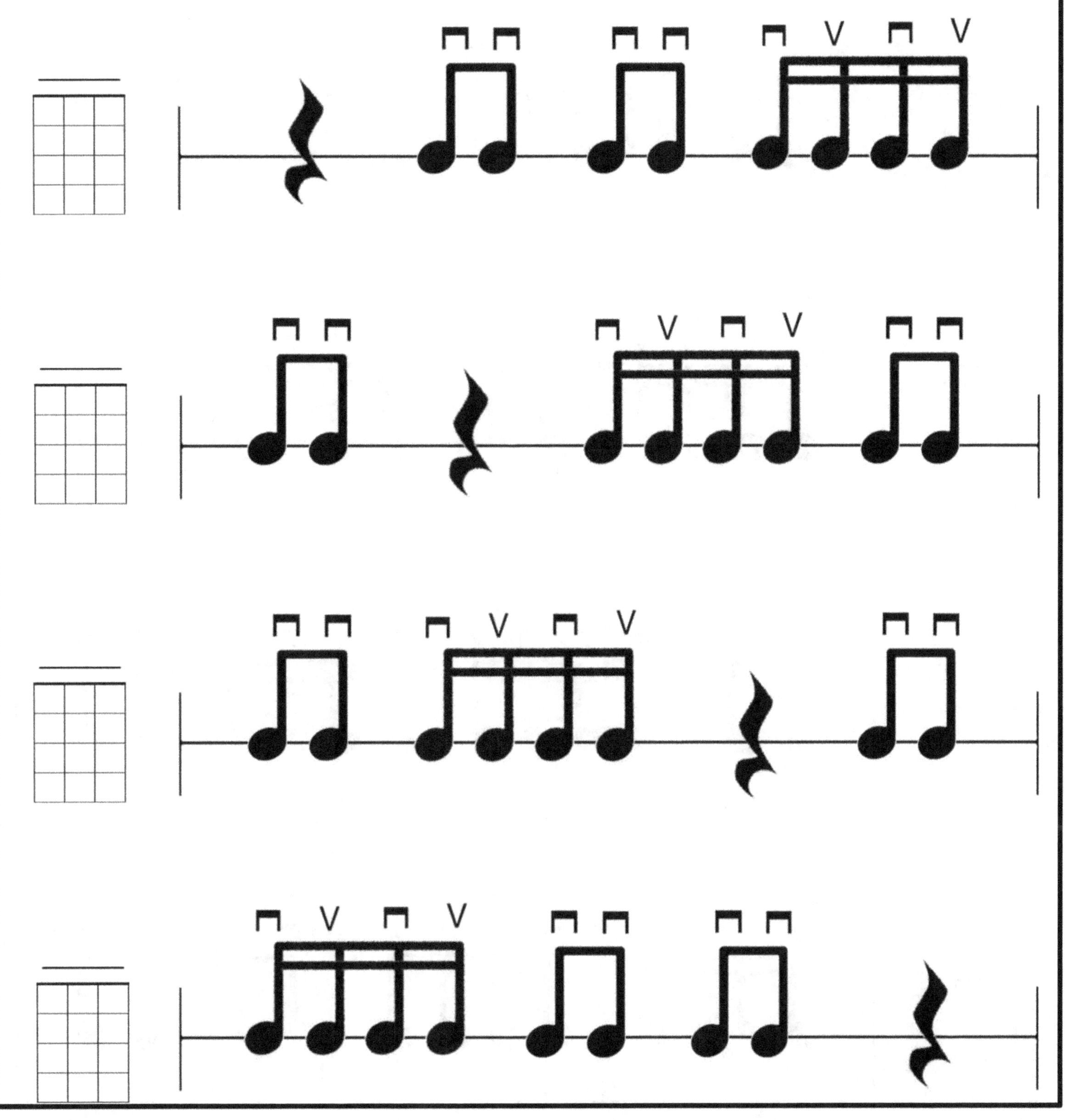

Strumming Exercises
Strum the rhythms below.

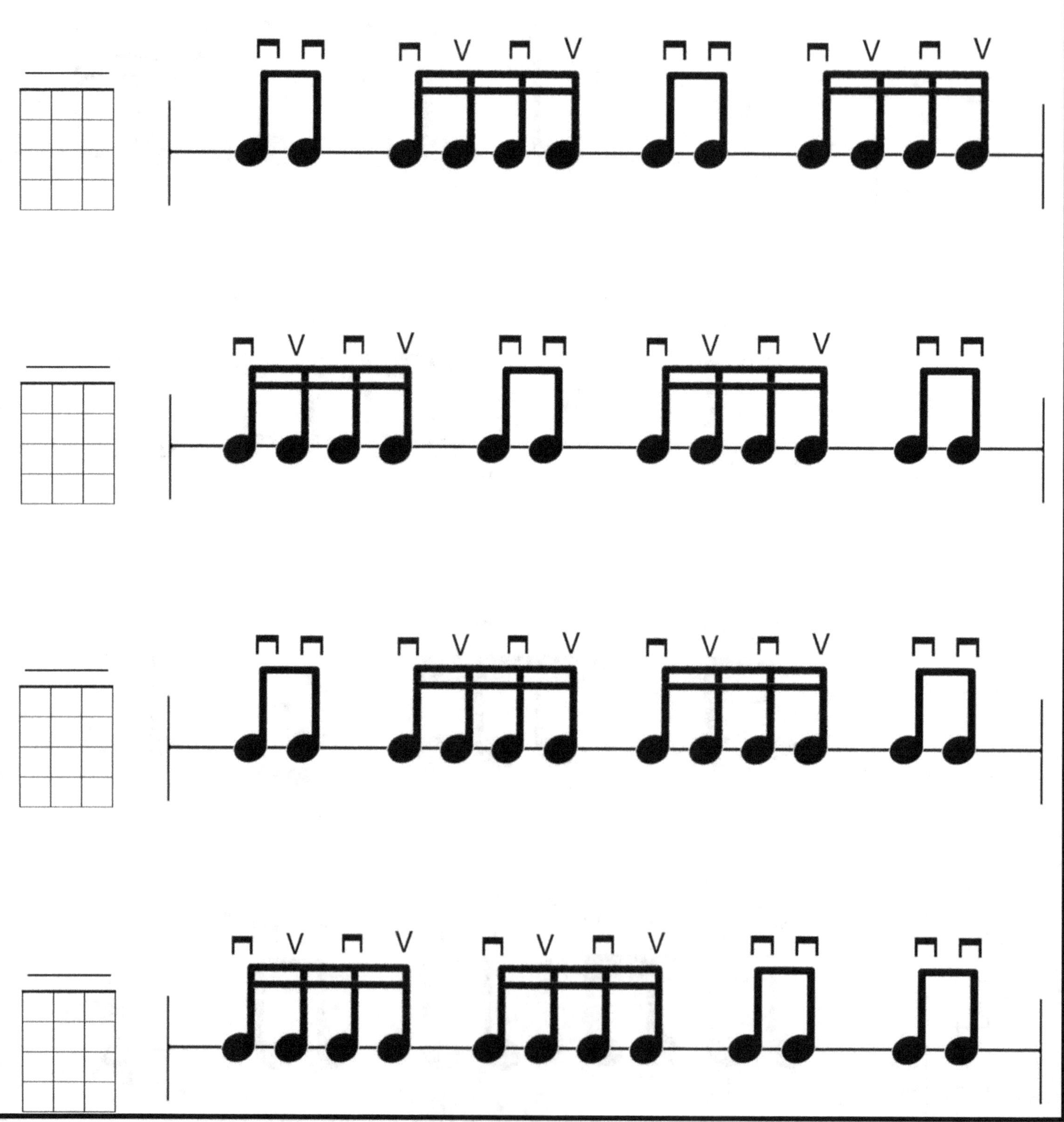

Strumming Exercises
Strum the rhythms below.

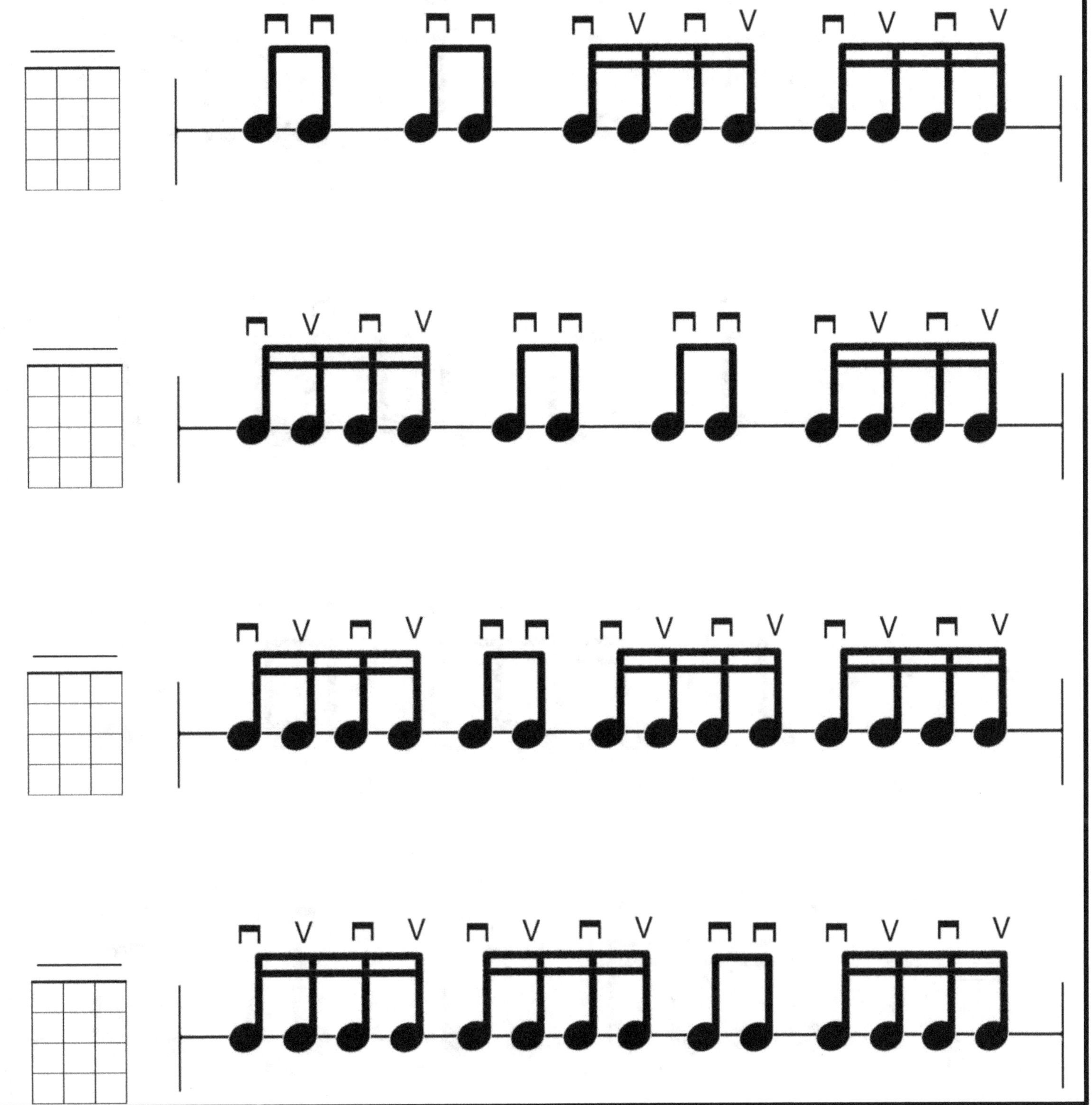

Strumming Exercises
Strum the rhythms below.

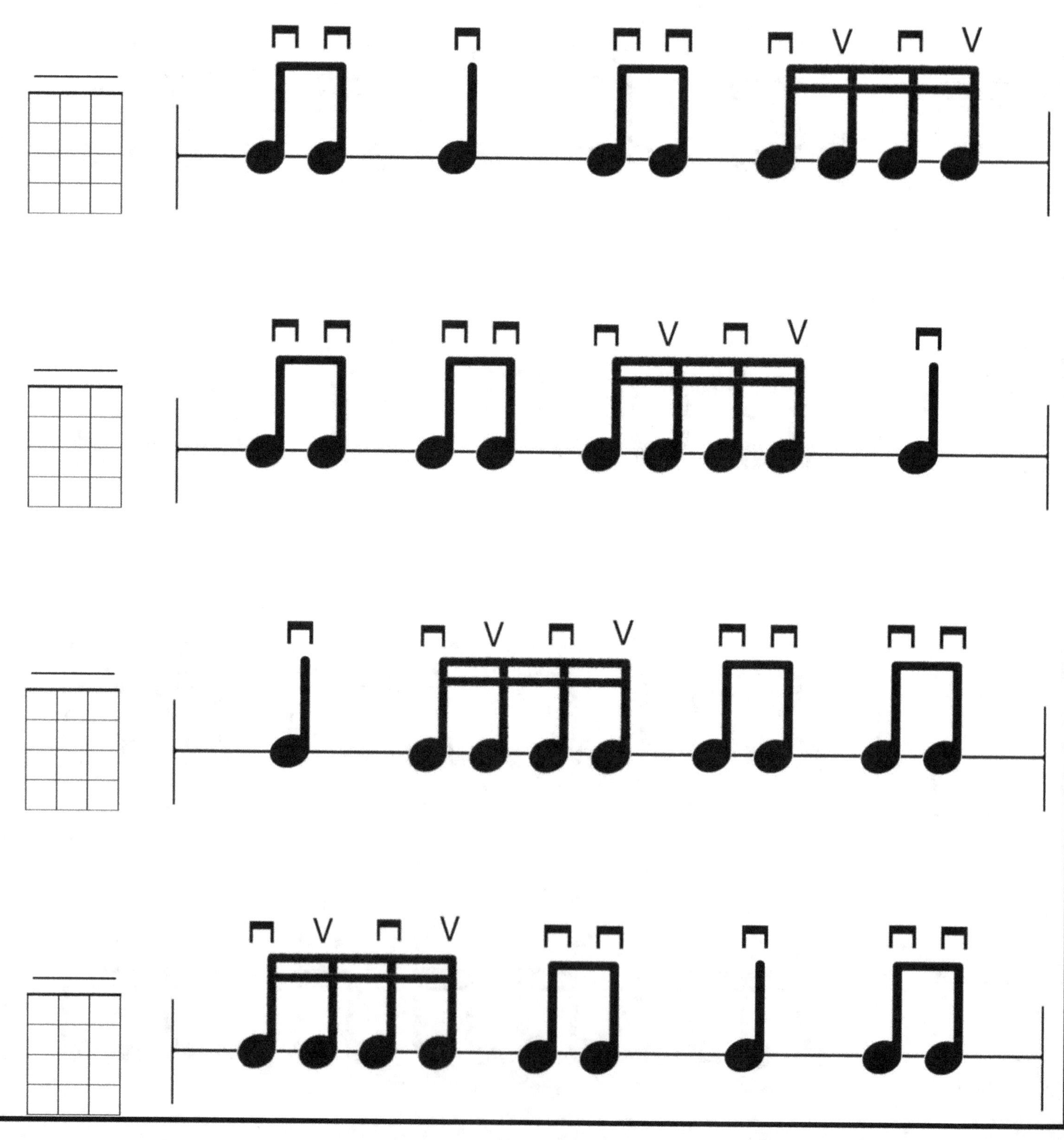

Strumming Exercises
Strum the rhythms below.

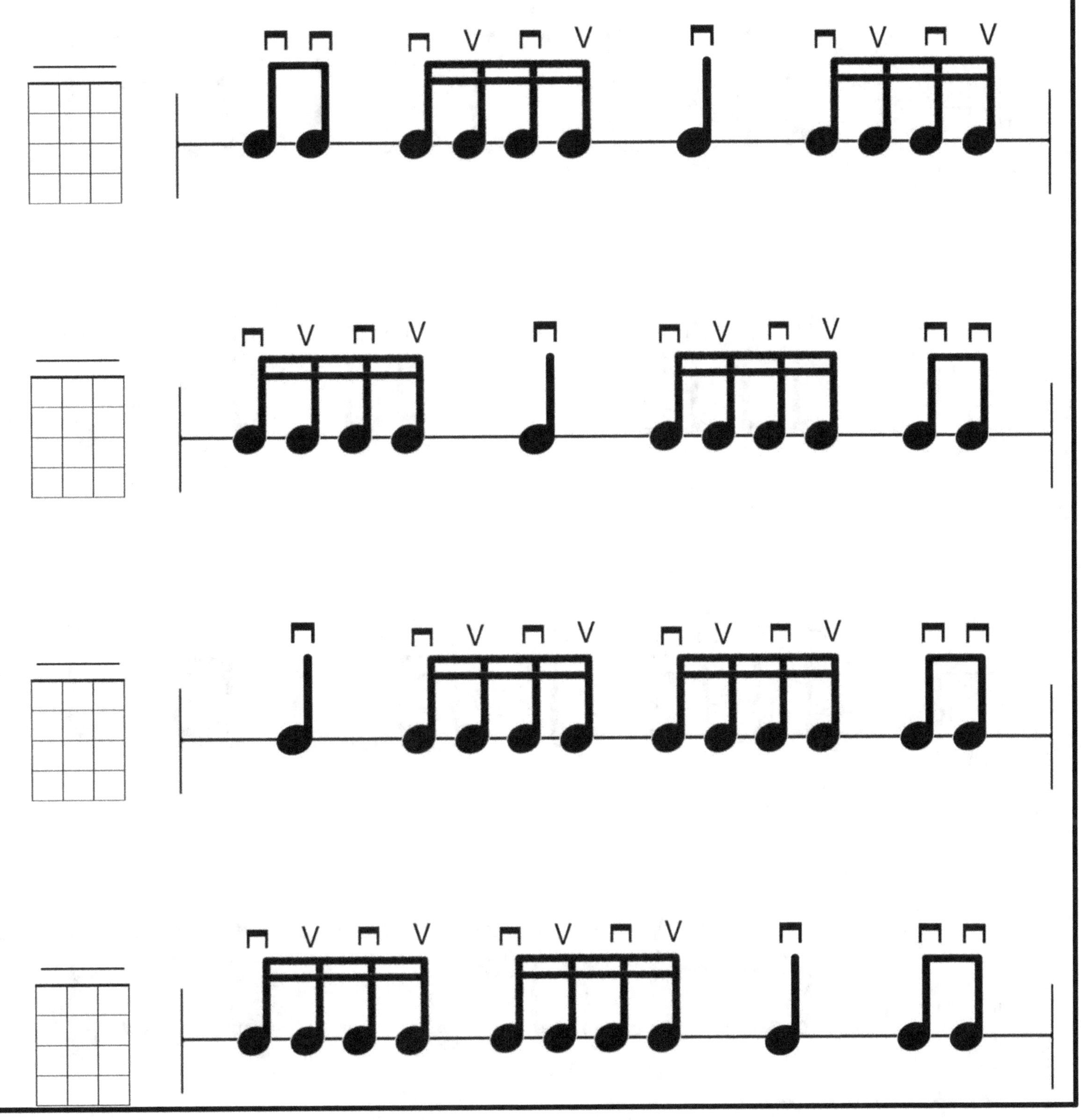

Strumming Exercises
Strum the rhythms below.

Strumming Exercises

Strum the rhythms below.

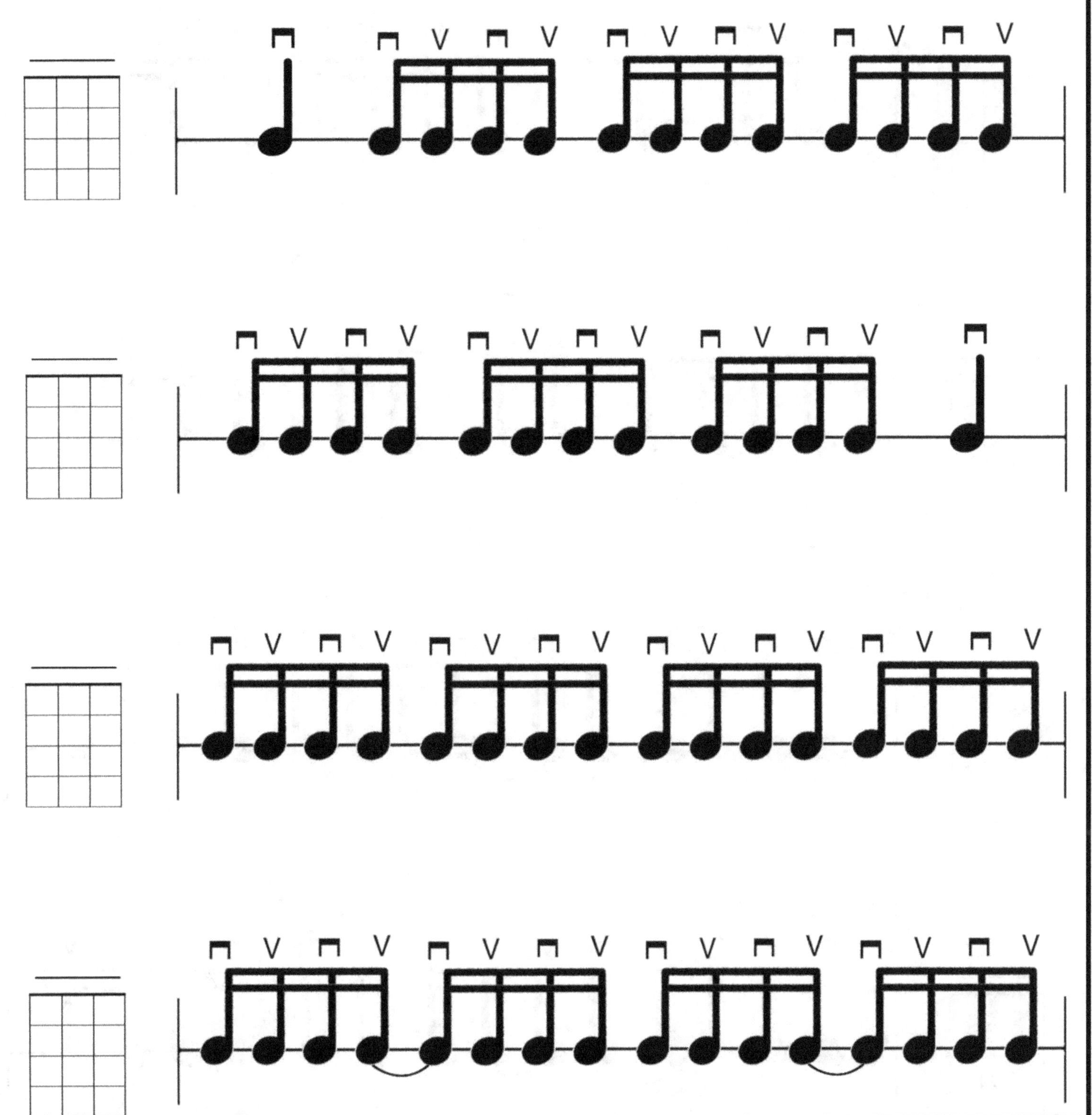

Strumming Exercises

Strum the rhythms below.

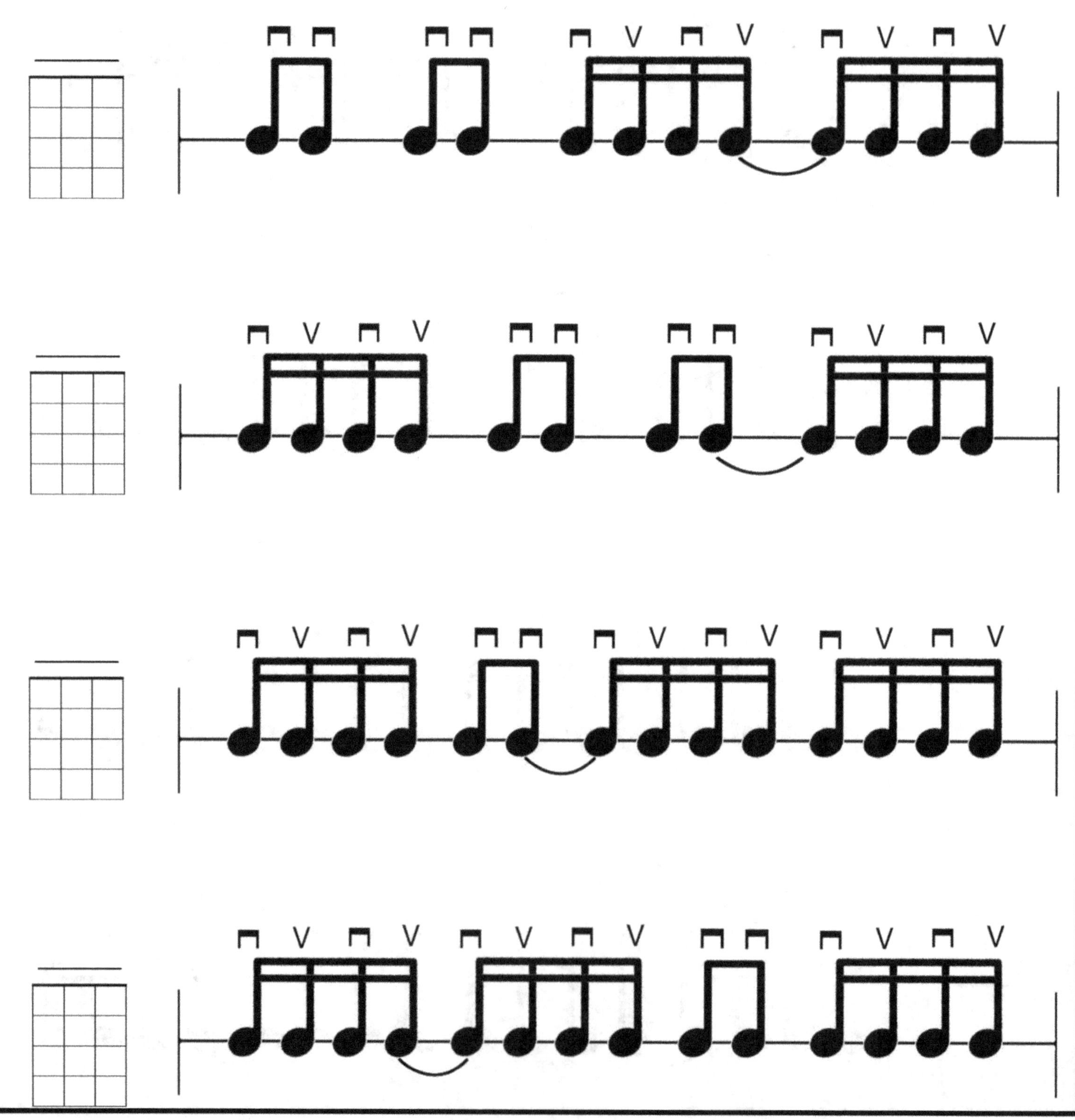

Strumming Exercises
Strum the rhythms below.

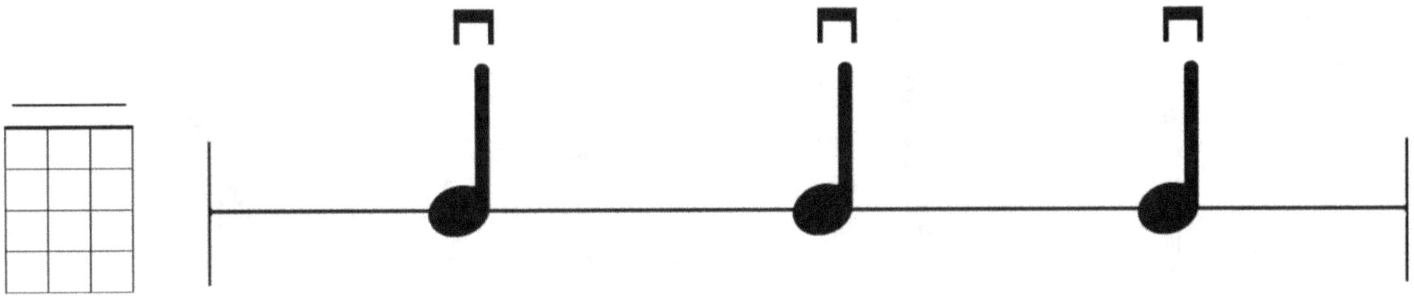

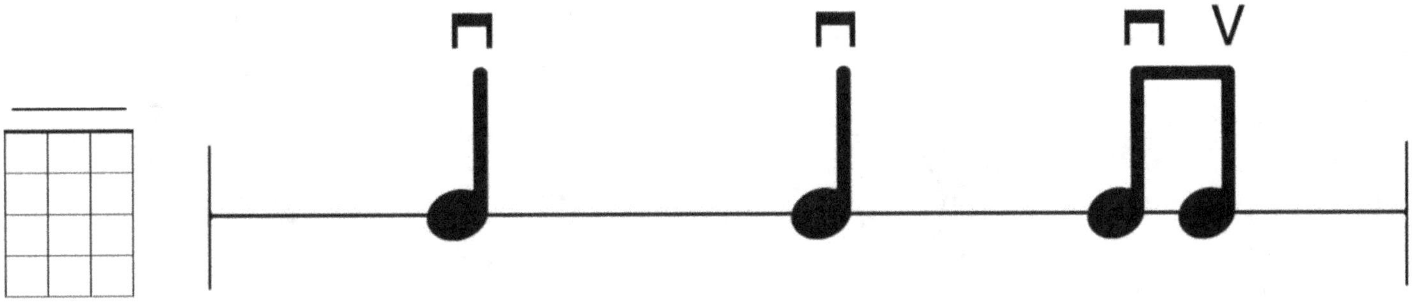

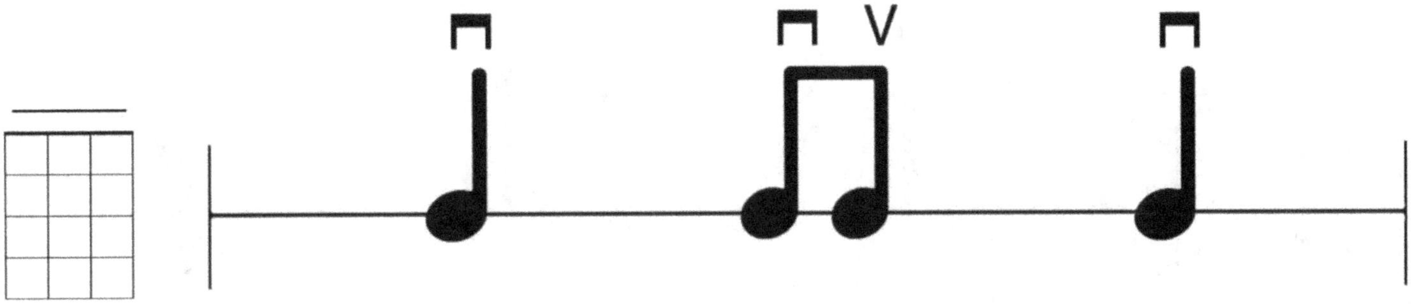

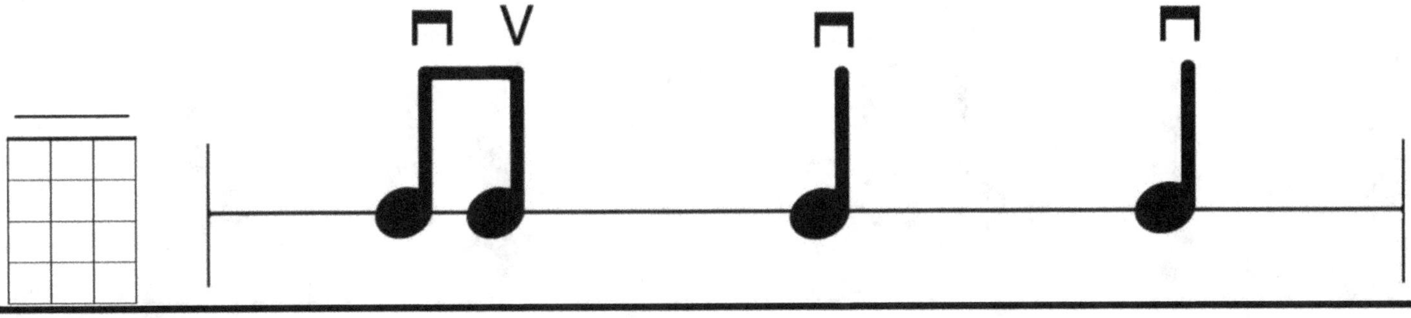

Strumming Exercises

Strum the rhythms below.

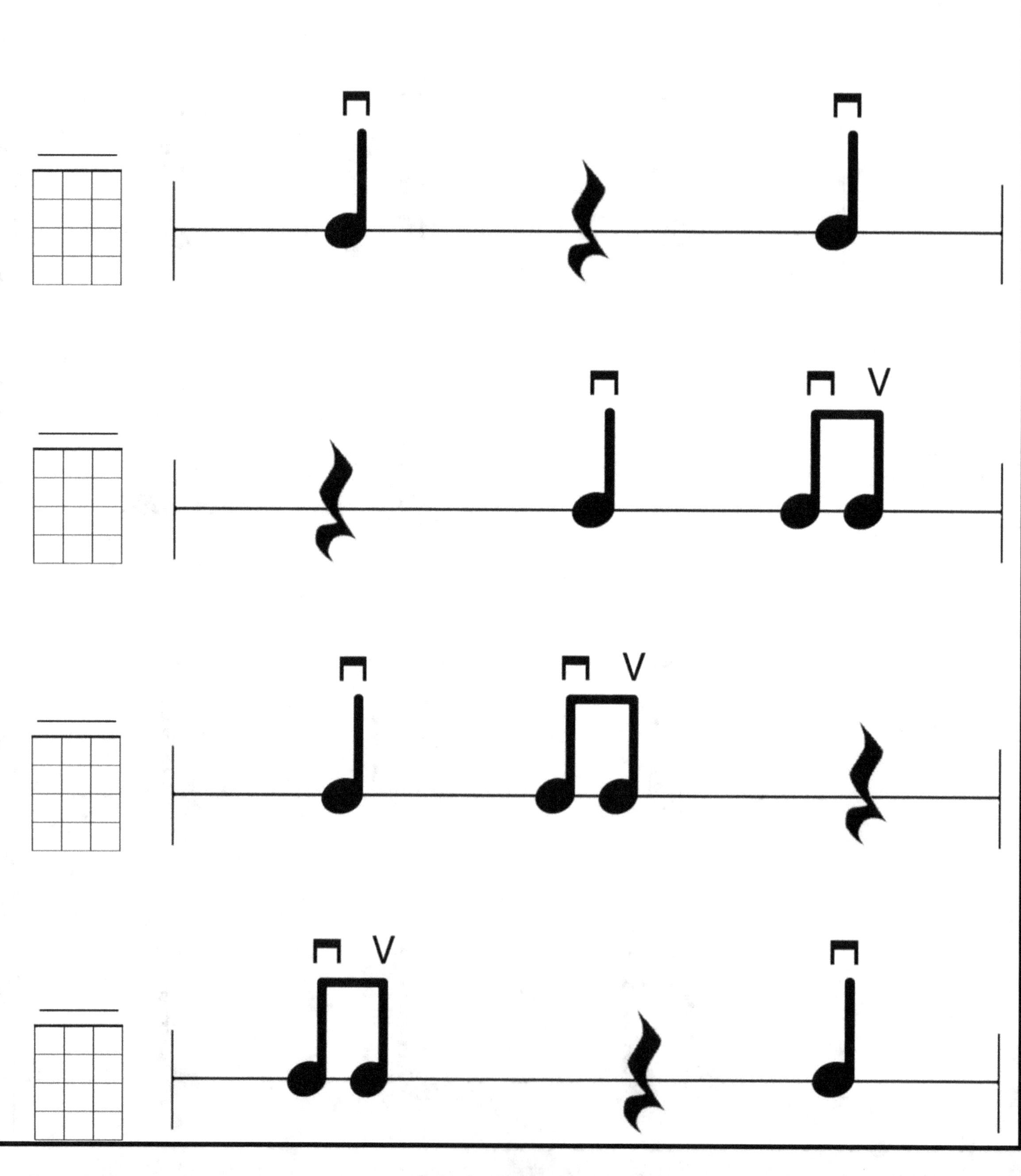

Strumming Exercises

Strum the rhythms below.

Strumming Exercises
Strum the rhythms below.

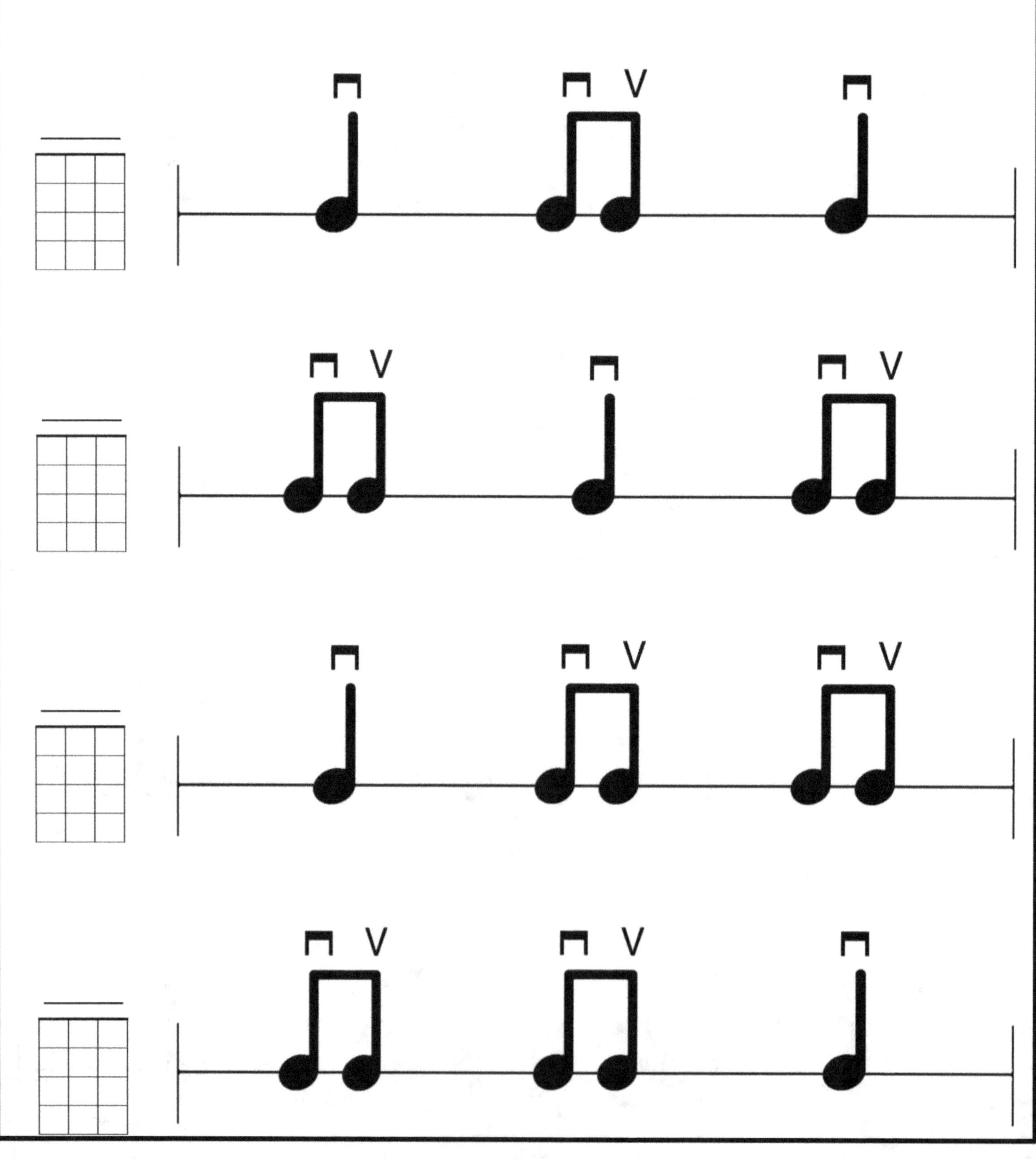

Strumming Exercises
Strum the rhythms below.

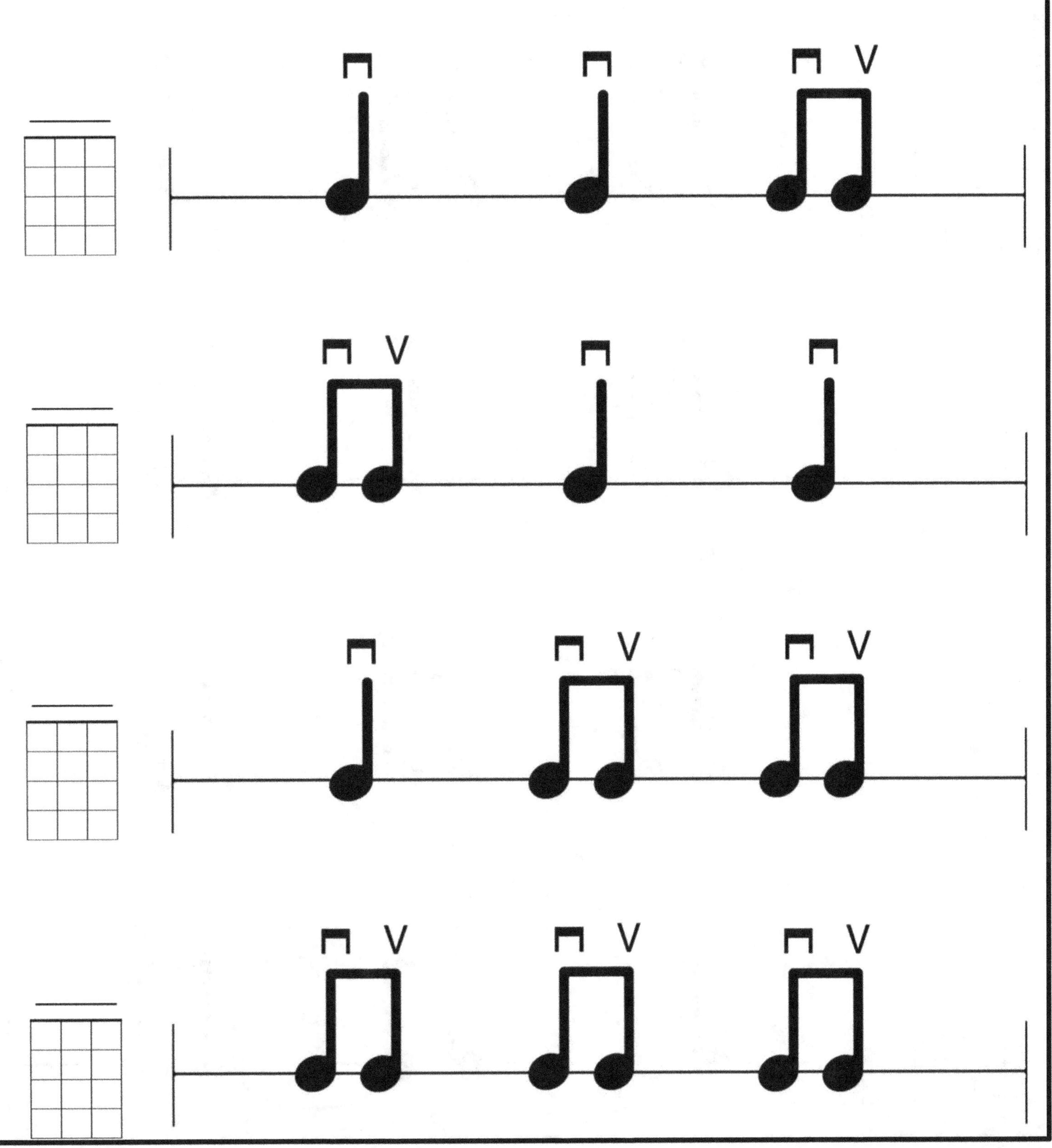

Strumming Exercises
Strum the rhythms below.

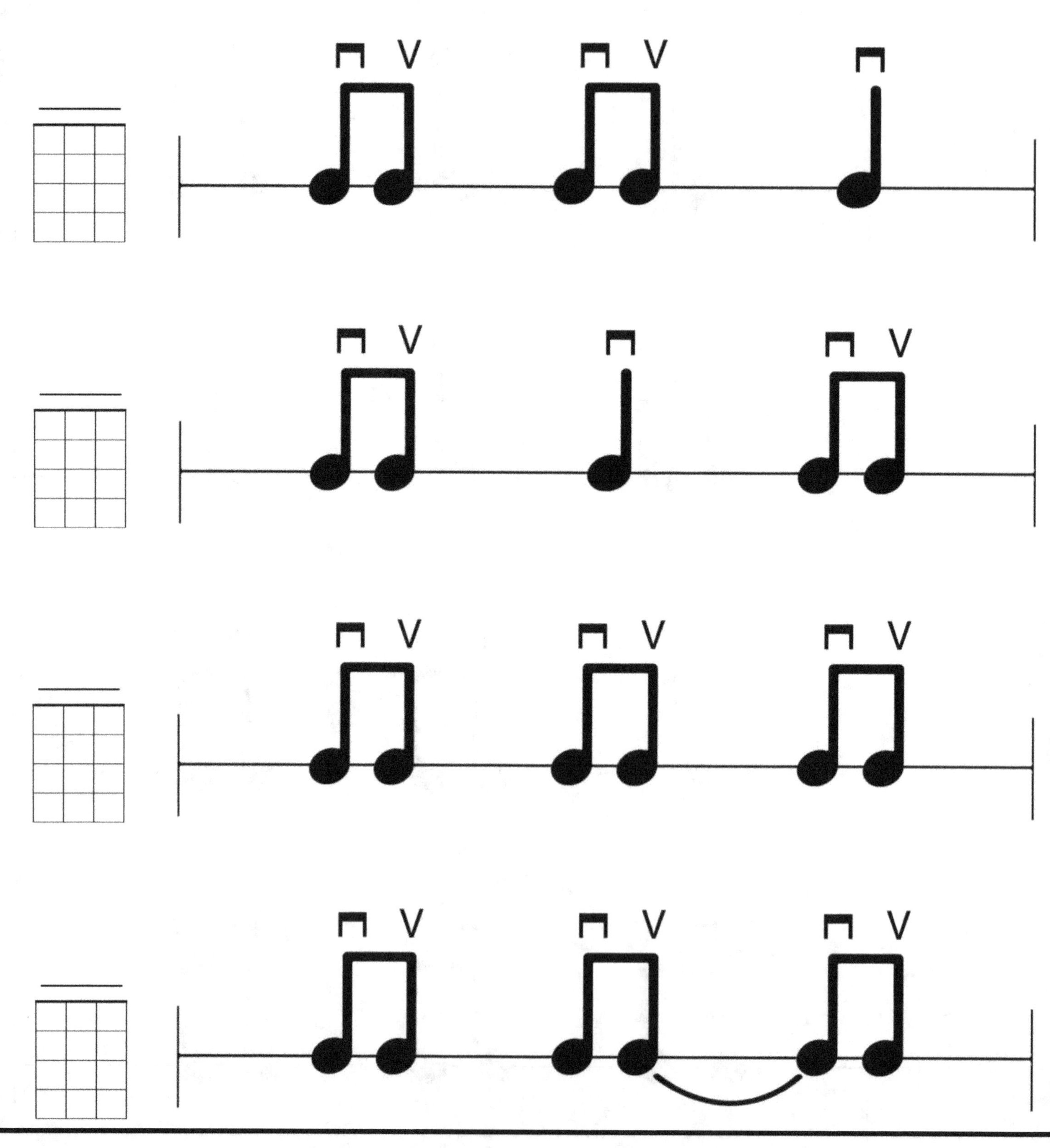

Strumming Exercises

Strum the rhythms below.

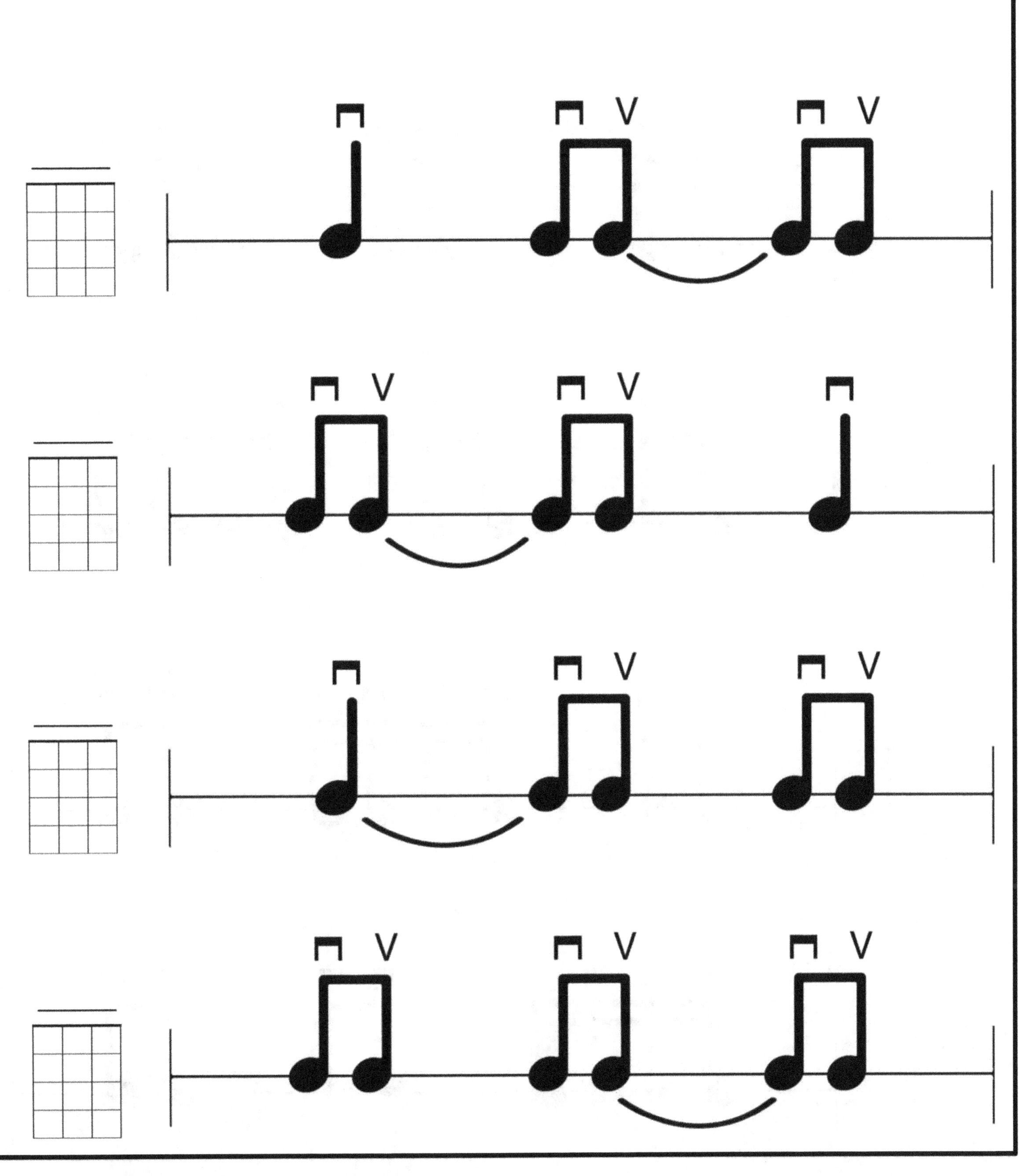

Strumming Exercises
Strum the rhythms below.

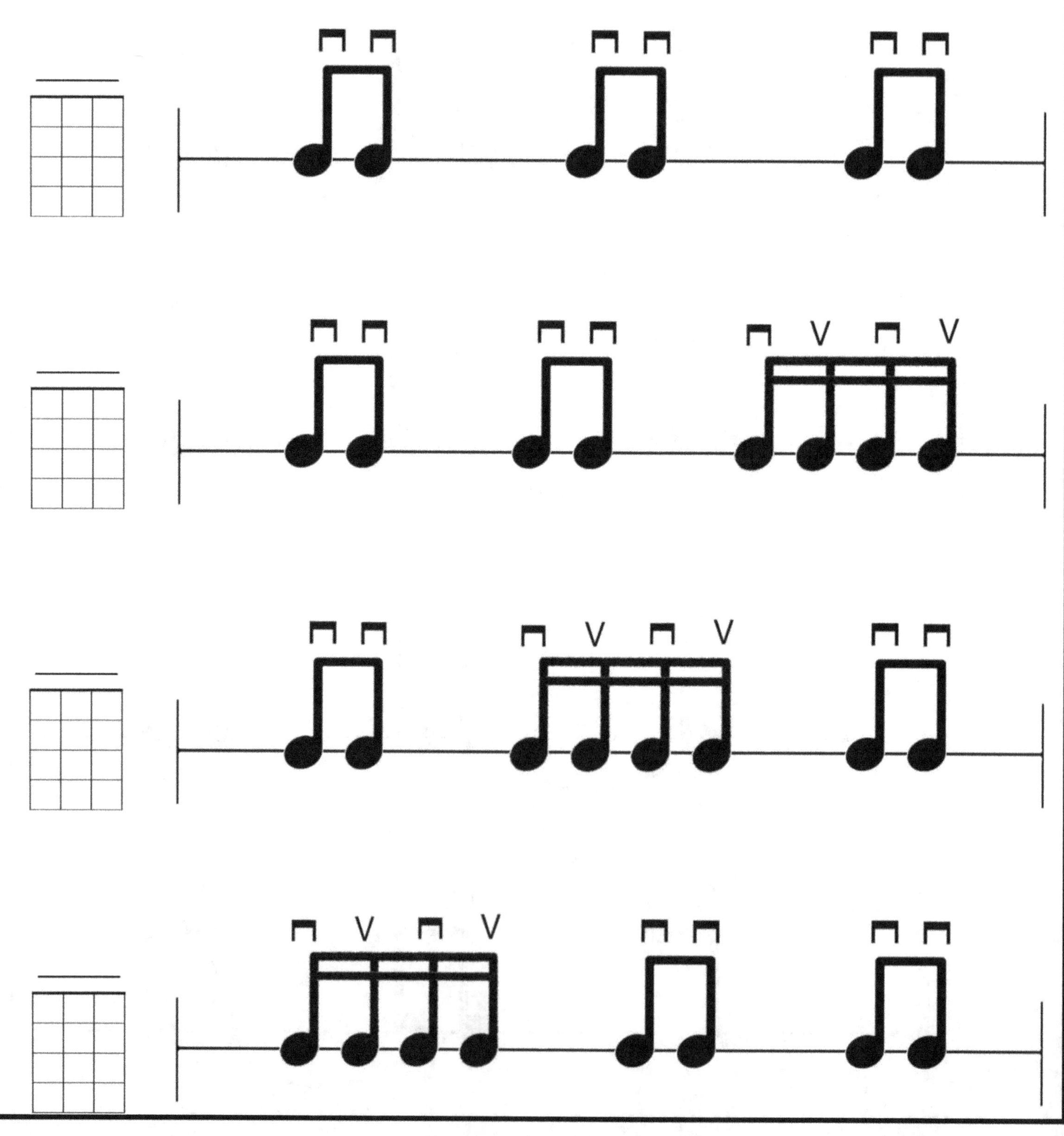

Strumming Exercises
Strum the rhythms below.

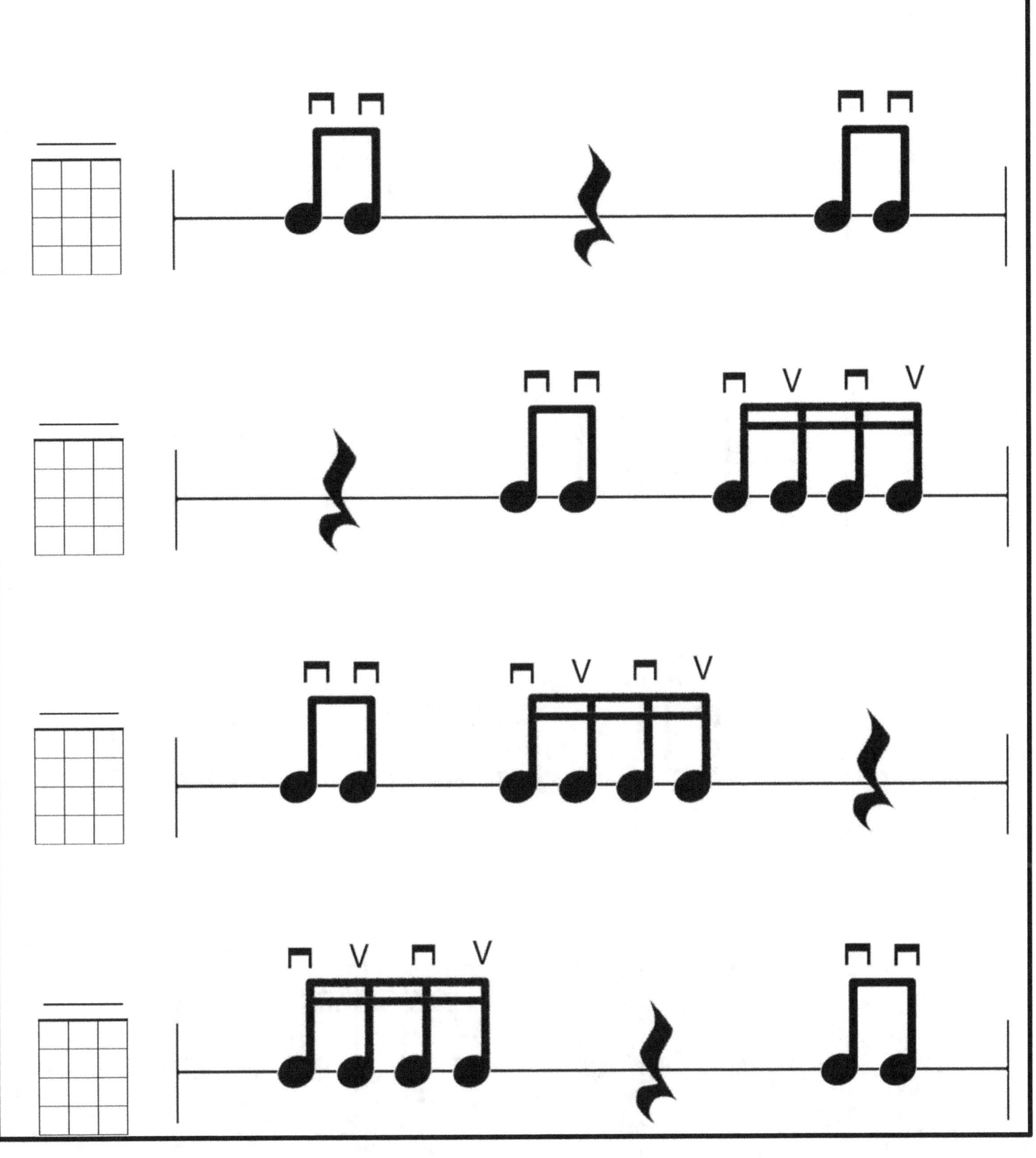

Strumming Exercises

Strum the rhythms below.

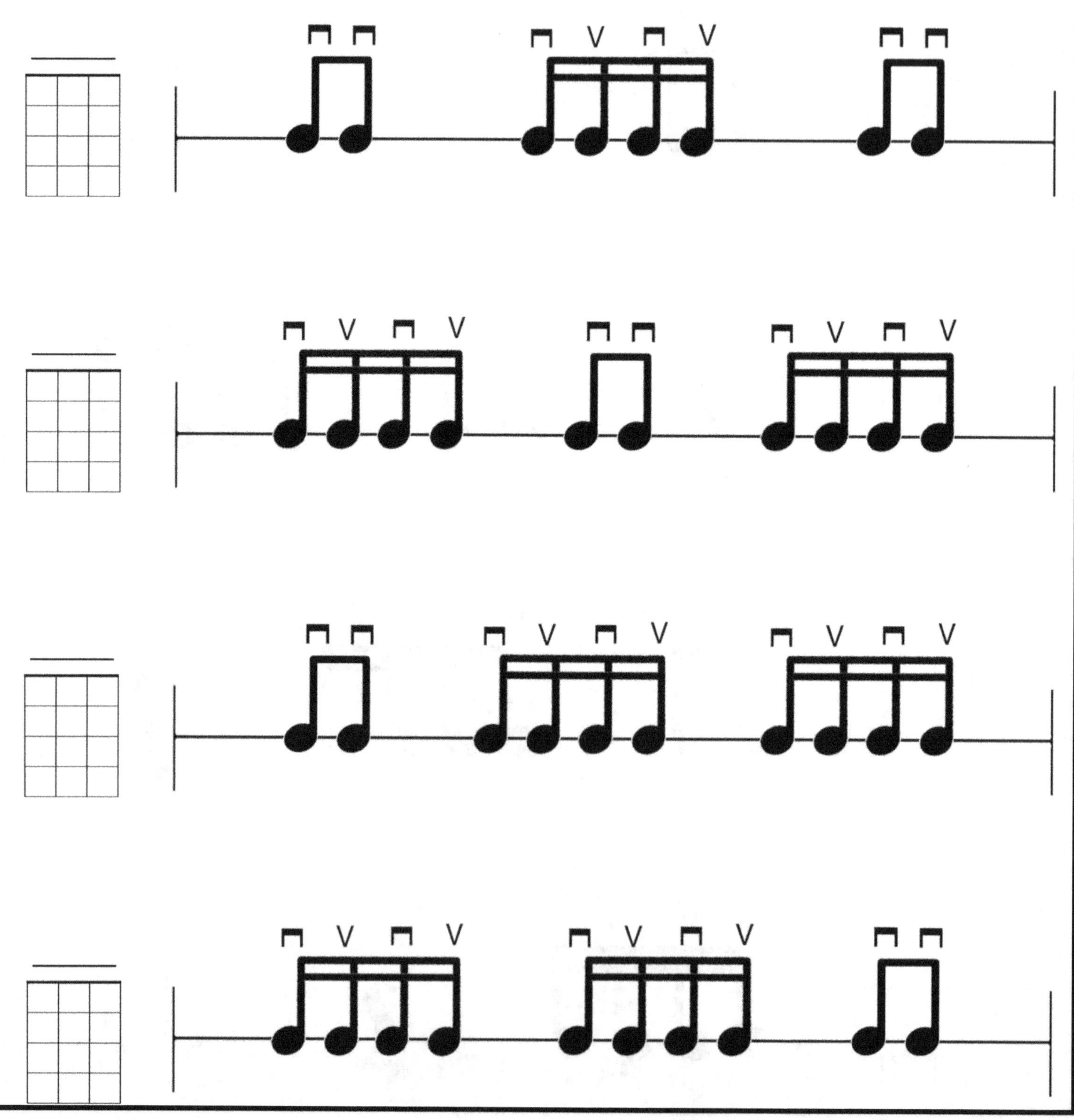

Strumming Exercises
Strum the rhythms below.

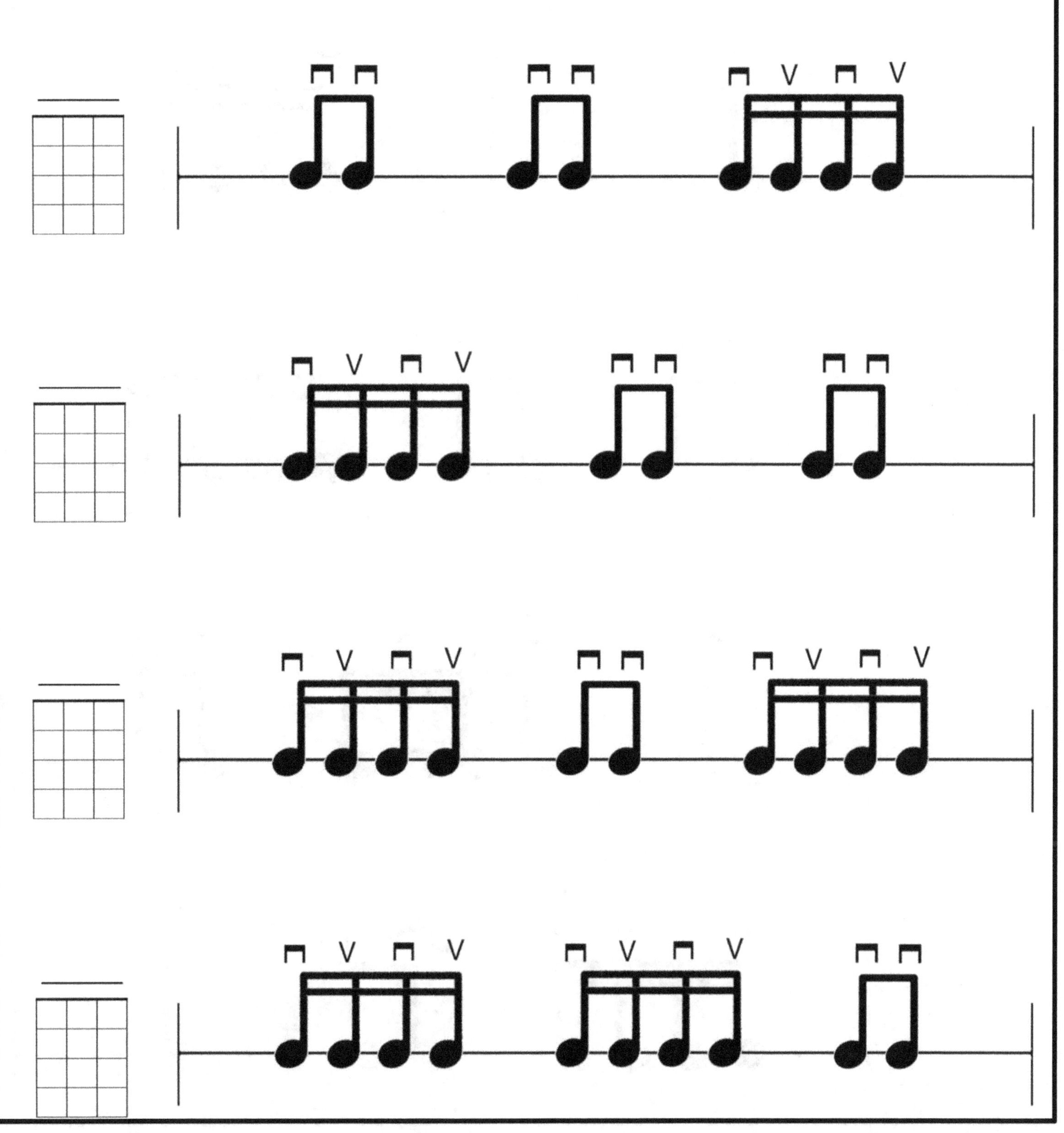

Strumming Exercises
Strum the rhythms below.

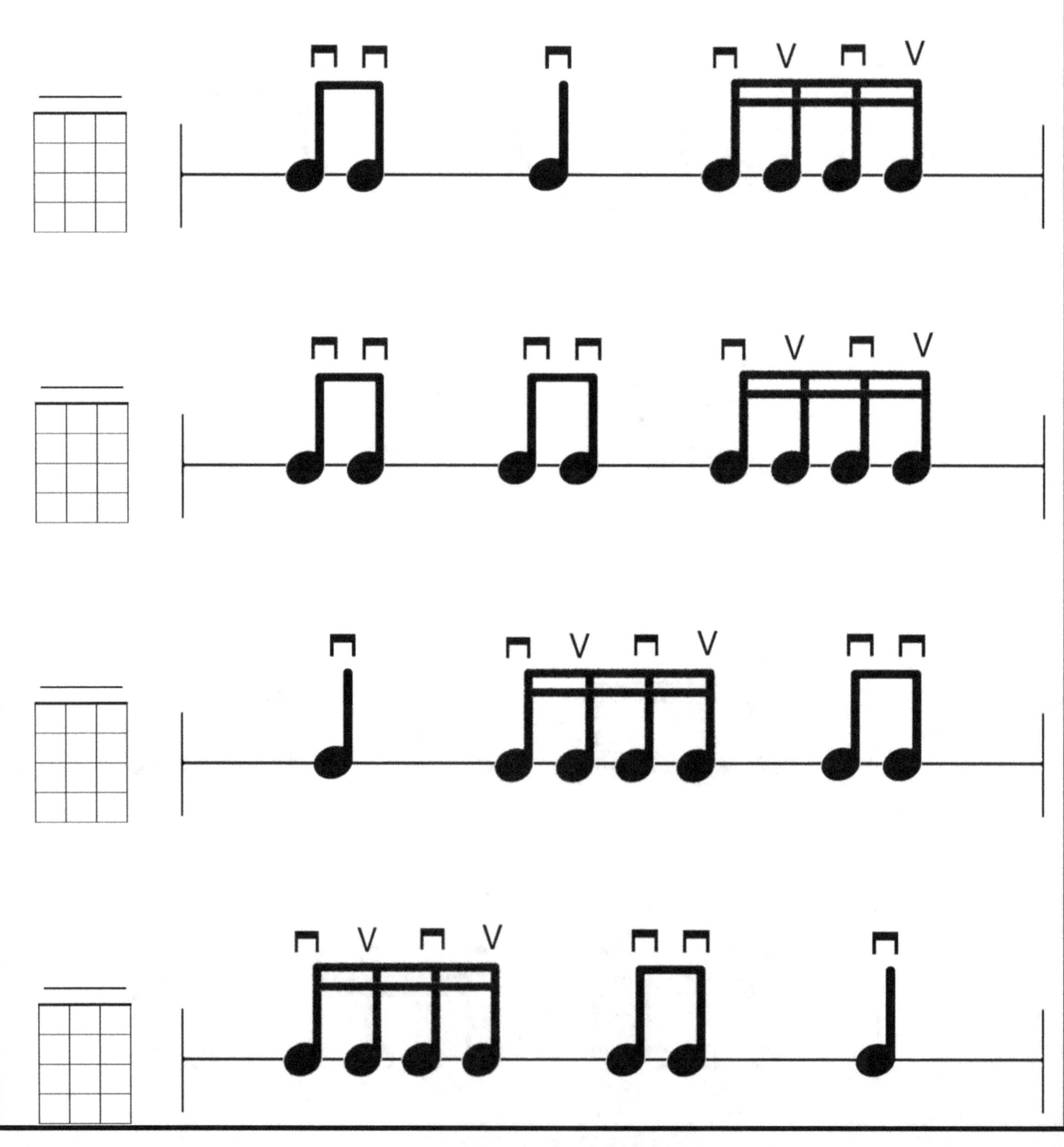

Strumming Exercises
Strum the rhythms below.

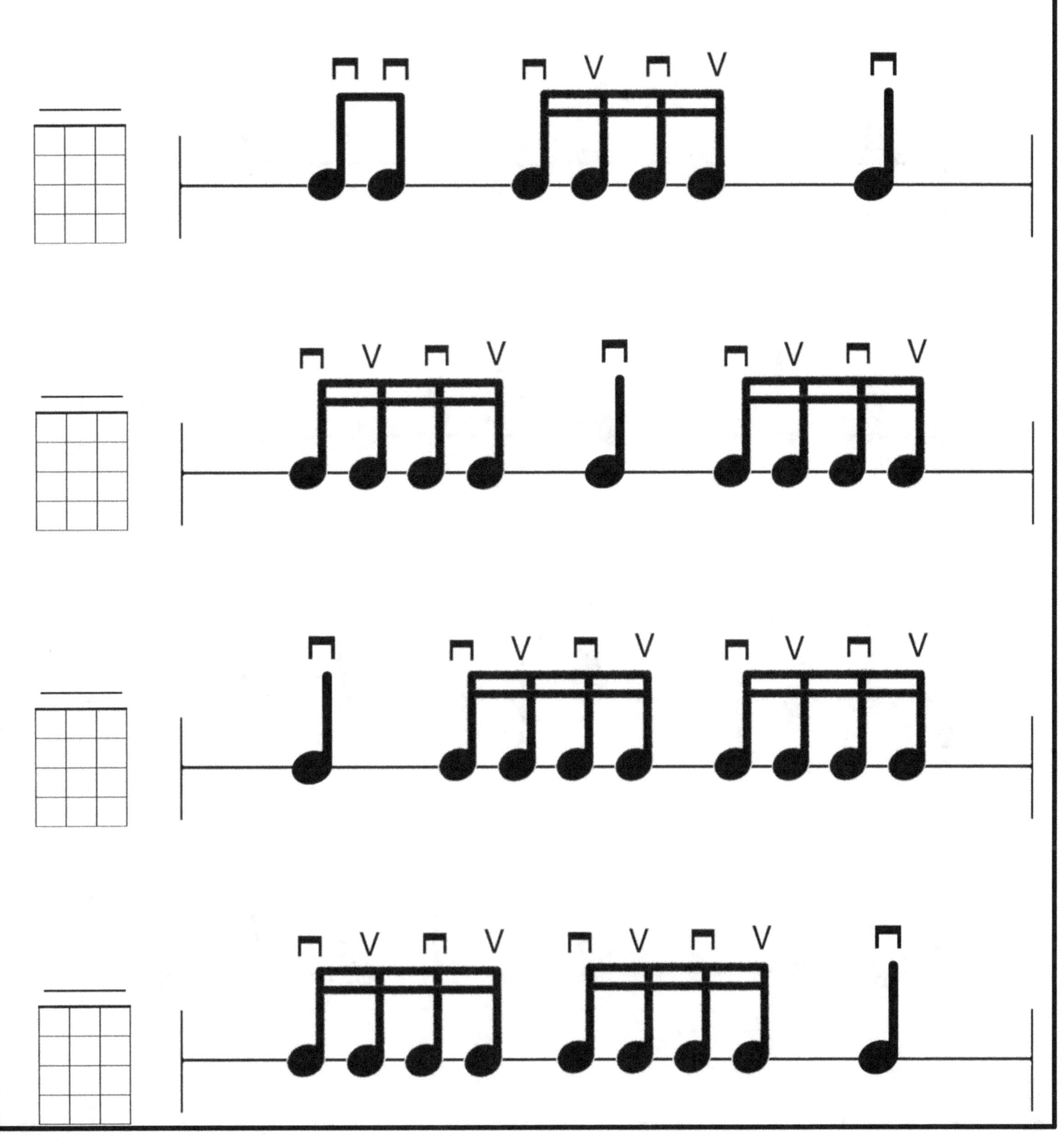

Quarter Rests Studies

Clap the rhythms below without clapping on the quarter rests.

Quarter Rests Studies

Clap the rhythms below without clapping on the quarter rests.

Quarter Rests Studies

Clap the rhythms below without clapping on the quarter rests.

Quarter Rests Studies

Clap the rhythms below without clapping on the quarter rests.

Quarter Rests Studies

Clap the rhythms below without clapping on the quarter rests.

Quarter Rests Studies

Clap the rhythms below without clapping on the quarter rests.

Quarter Rests Studies

Clap the rhythms below without clapping on the quarter rests.

Quarter Rests Studies

Clap the rhythms below without clapping on the quarter rests.

Quarter Rests Studies

Clap the rhythms below without clapping on the quarter rests.

Quarter Rests Studies

Clap the rhythms below without clapping on the quarter rests.

Quarter Rests Studies

Clap the rhythms below without clapping on the quarter rests.

Quarter Rests Studies

Clap the rhythms below without clapping on the quarter rests.

Quarter Rests Studies

Clap the rhythms below without clapping on the quarter rests.

Strum Pattern Composition

Use the rhythms to compose strum patterns for each example.

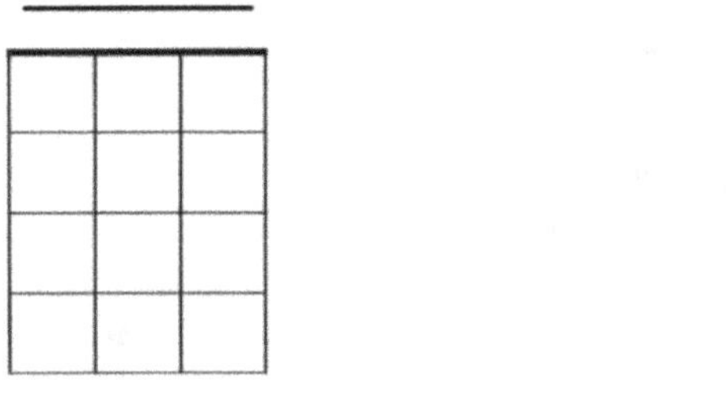

$\frac{4}{4}$

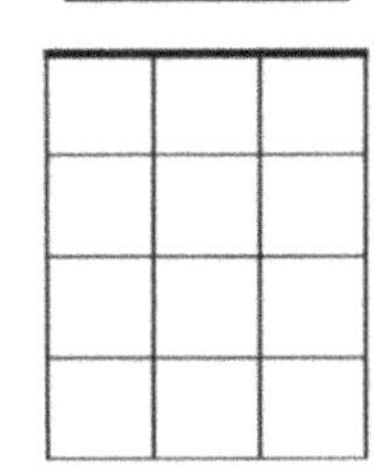

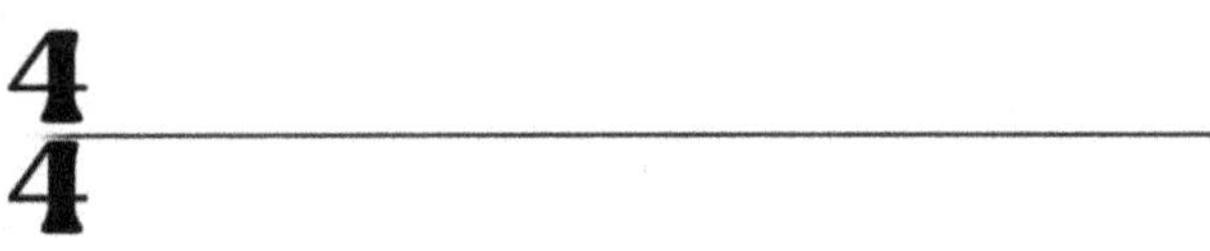

$\frac{4}{4}$

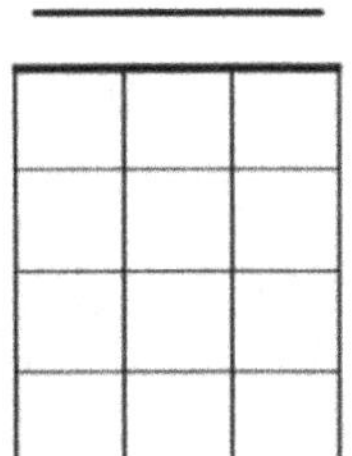

$\frac{4}{4}$

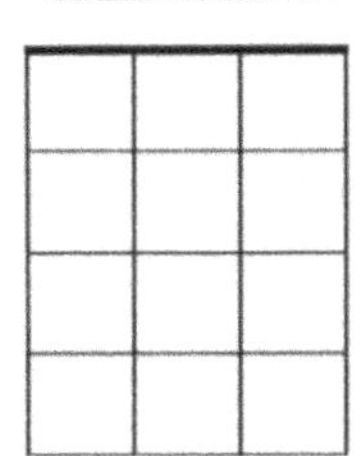

$\frac{4}{4}$

Strum Pattern Composition

Use the rhythms to compose strum patterns for each example.

Strum Pattern Composition

Use the rhythms to compose strum patterns for each example.

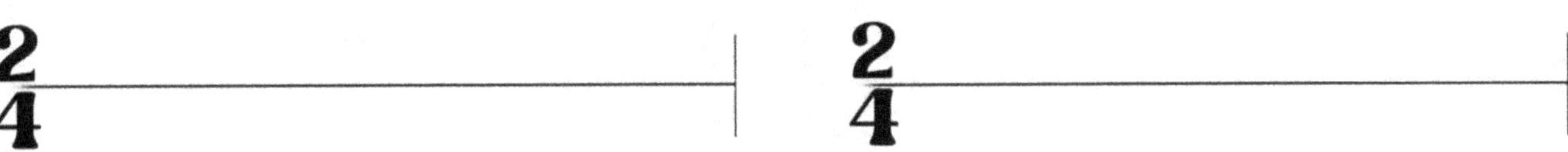

Strum Pattern Composition

Use the rhythms to
compose strum patterns
for each example.

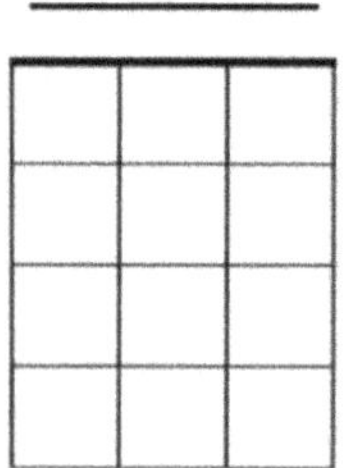

$\frac{4}{4}$

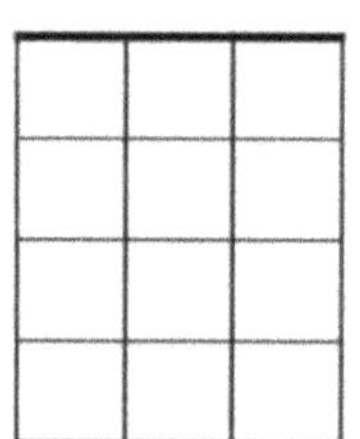

$\frac{4}{4}$

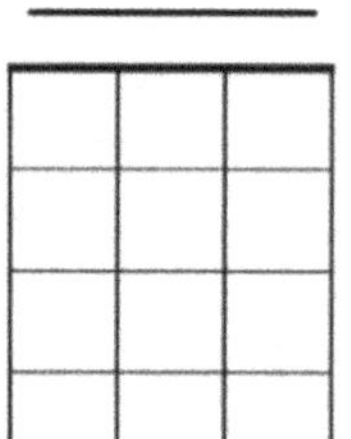

$\frac{4}{4}$

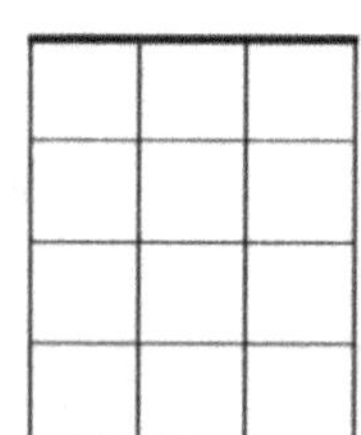

$\frac{4}{4}$

Strum Pattern Composition

Use the rhythms to
compose strum patterns
for each example.

Quarter
Notes

Eighth
Notes

Ties

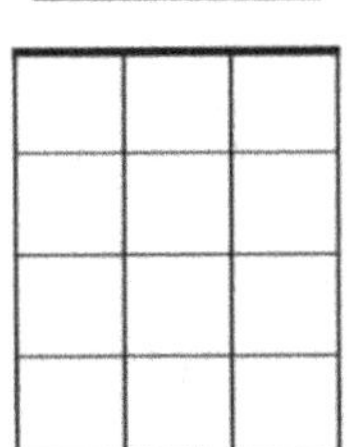

$\frac{3}{4}$ 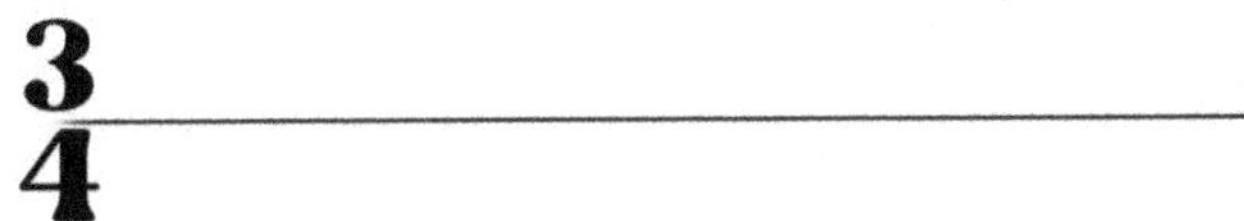

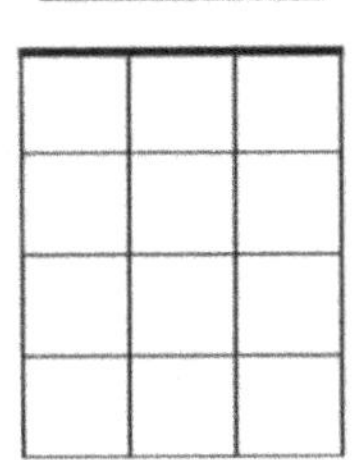

$\frac{3}{4}$ 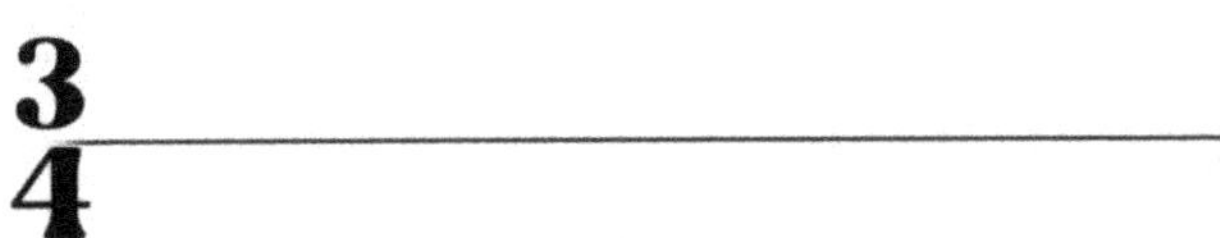

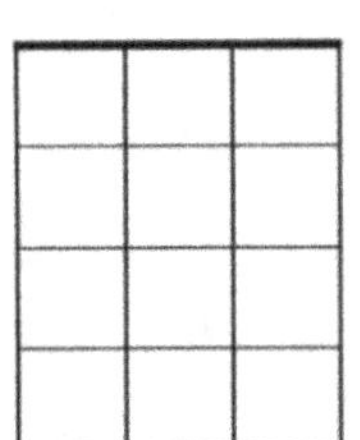

$\frac{3}{4}$

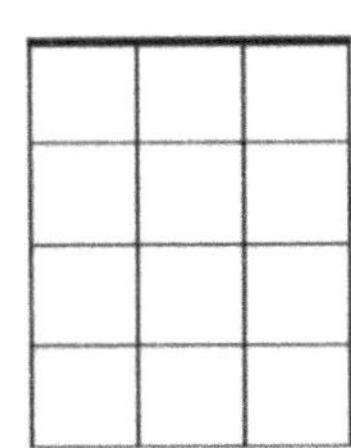

$\frac{3}{4}$ 

Strum Pattern Composition

Use the rhythms to
compose strum patterns
for each example.

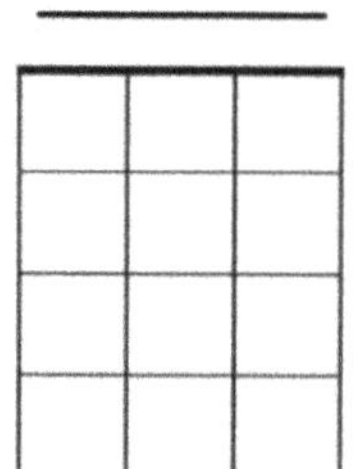

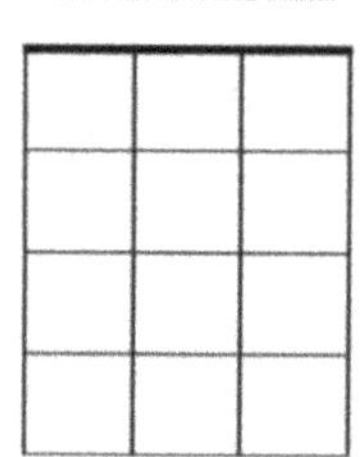

$\frac{2}{4}$

$\frac{2}{4}$

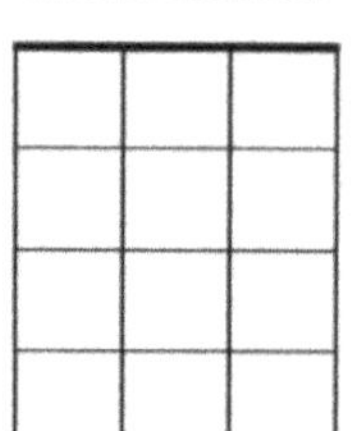

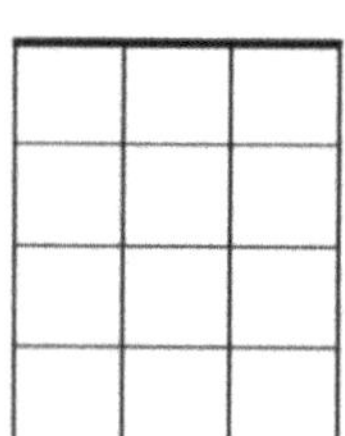

$\frac{2}{4}$

$\frac{2}{4}$

Strum Pattern Composition

Use the rhythms to
compose strum patterns
for each example.

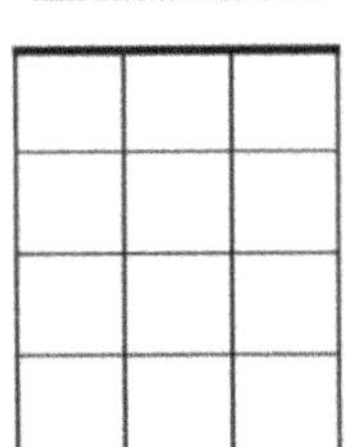

Quarter
Notes

Eighth
Notes

Sixteenth
Notes

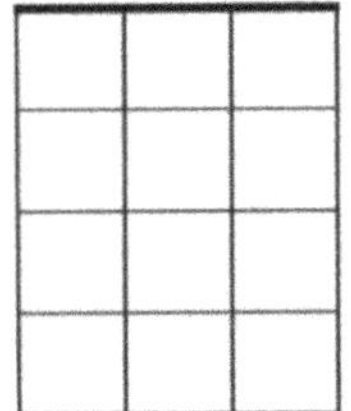

$\frac{4}{4}$

$\frac{4}{4}$

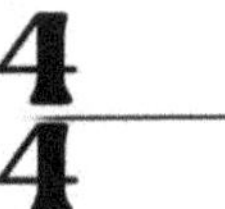

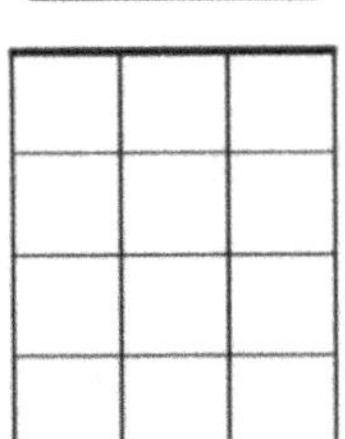

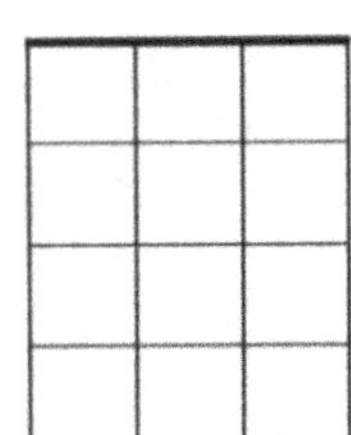

$\frac{4}{4}$

$\frac{4}{4}$

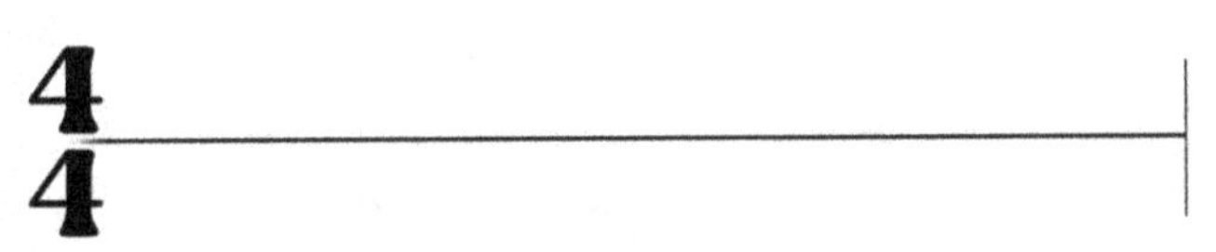

Strum Pattern Composition

Use the rhythms to
compose strum patterns
for each example.

Quarter
Notes

Eighth
Notes

Sixteenth
Notes

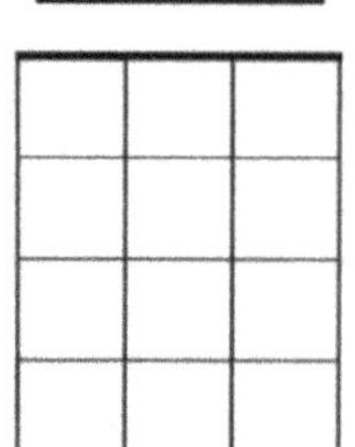

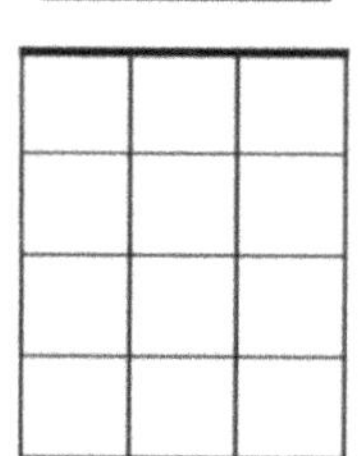

$\frac{3}{4}$

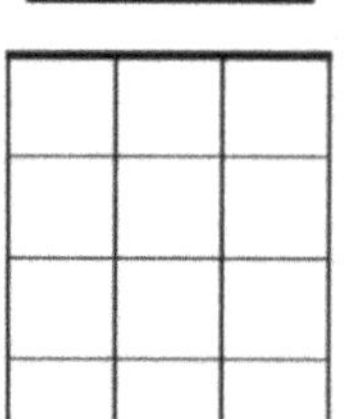

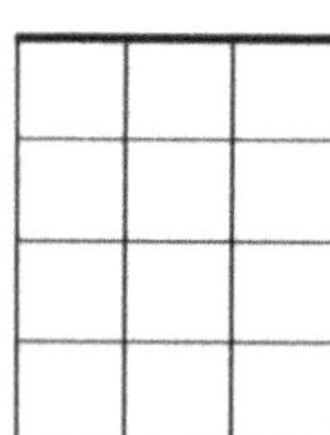

$\frac{3}{4}$

Strum Pattern Composition

Use the rhythms to
compose strum patterns
for each example.

Quarter
Notes

Eighth
Notes

Sixteenth
Notes

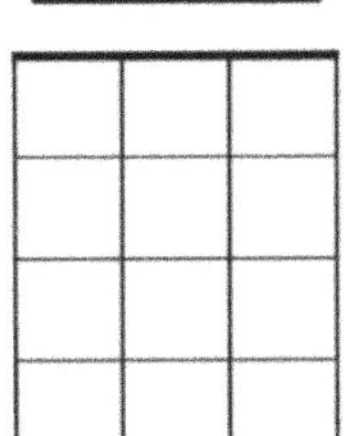

$\frac{2}{4}$ 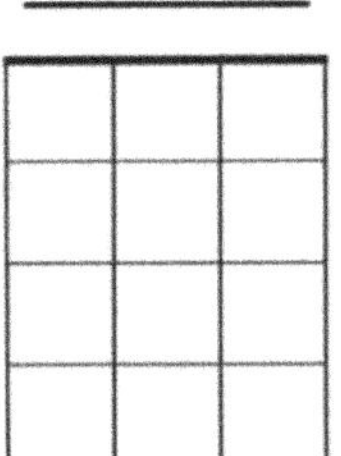

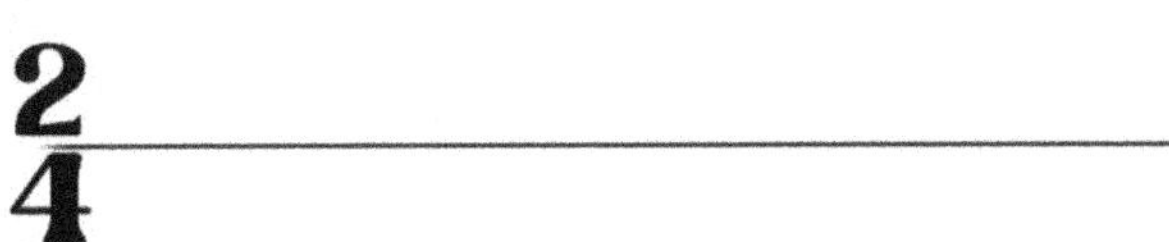

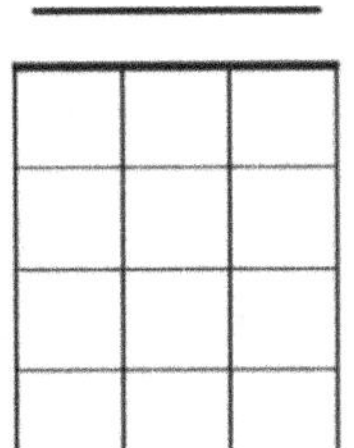

$\frac{2}{4}$ 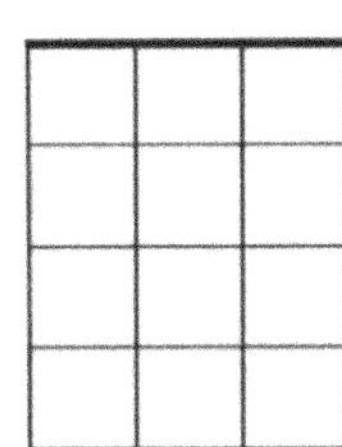

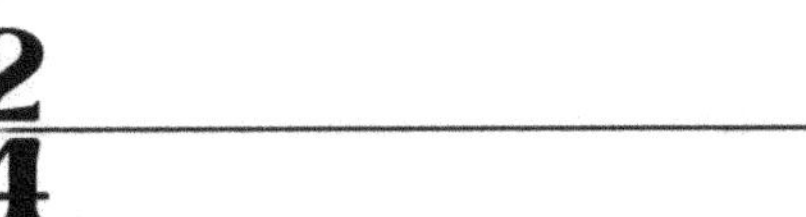

$\frac{2}{4}$

$\frac{2}{4}$

Strum Pattern Composition

Use the rhythms to
compose strum patterns
for each example.

Quarter
Notes

Eighth
Notes

Sixteenth
Notes

Ties

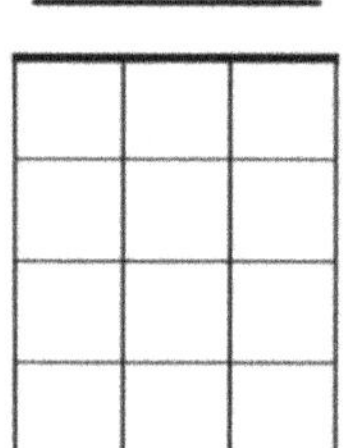

$\frac{4}{4}$ ______________________________|

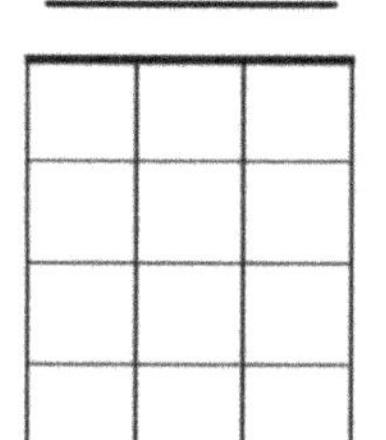

$\frac{4}{4}$ ______________________________|

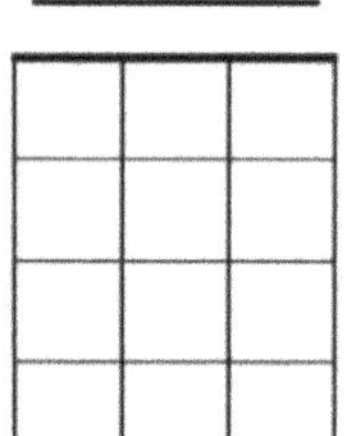

$\frac{4}{4}$ ______________________________|

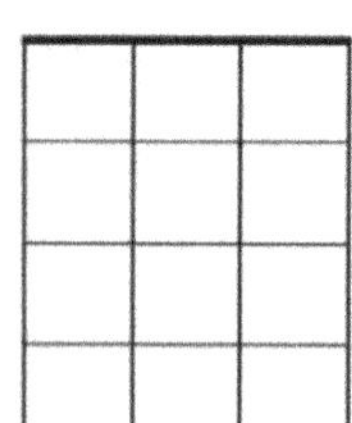

$\frac{4}{4}$ ______________________________|

Strum Pattern Composition

Use the rhythms to
compose strum patterns
for each example.

Quarter
Notes

Eighth
Notes

Sixteenth
Notes

Ties

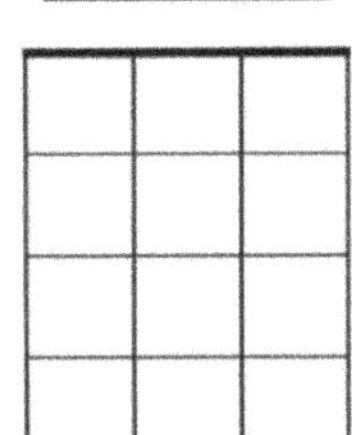

$\frac{3}{4}$

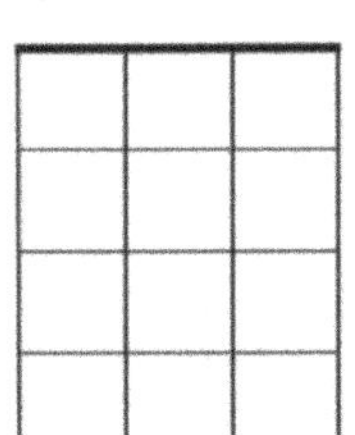

$\frac{3}{4}$

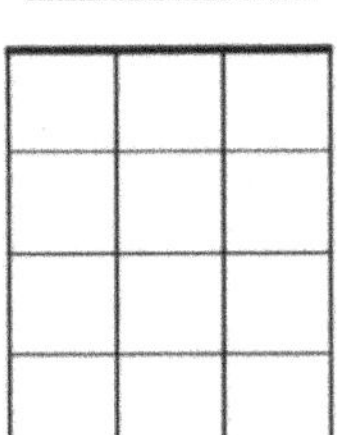

$\frac{3}{4}$

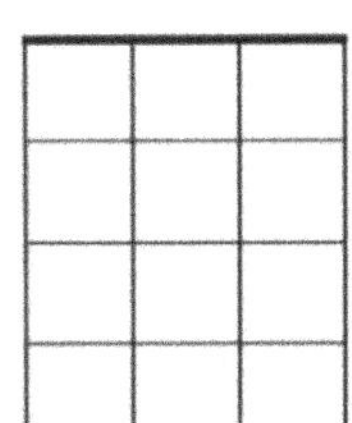

$\frac{3}{4}$

Strum Pattern Composition

Use the rhythms to
compose strum patterns
for each example.

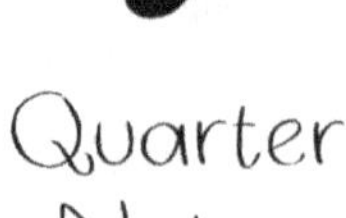

Quarter
Notes

Eighth
Notes

Sixteenth
Notes

Ties

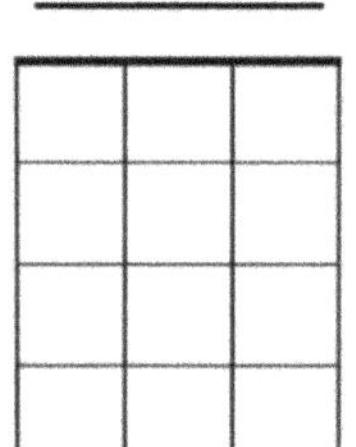

$\frac{2}{4}$

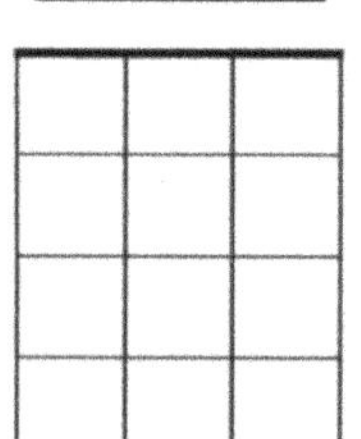

$\frac{2}{4}$

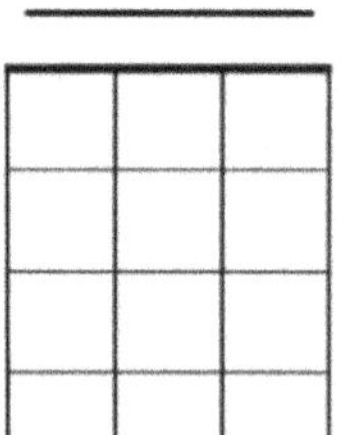

$\frac{2}{4}$

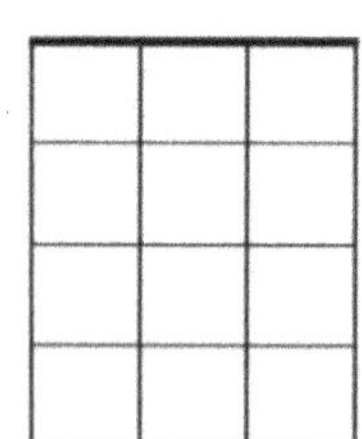

$\frac{2}{4}$

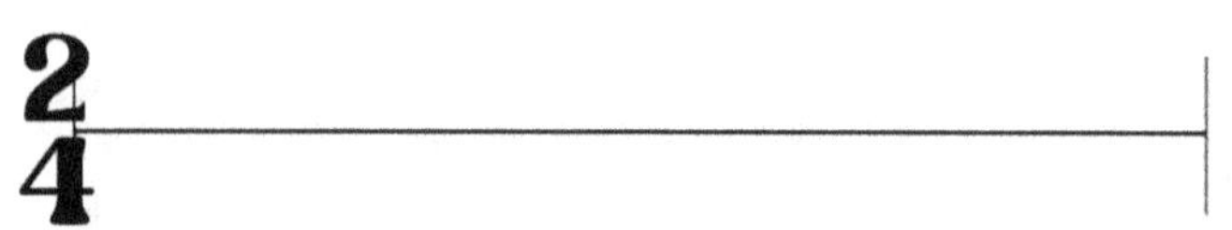

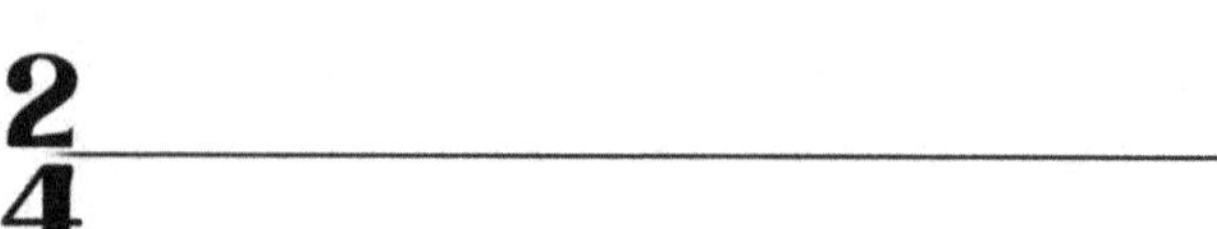

Congratulations on completing the Comprehensive Ukulele Strumming Workbook! You've embarked on a musical journey, mastering the essential rhythms and strumming patterns that form the backbone of countless songs. Keep strumming, keep exploring, and most importantly, keep having fun with your ukulele. Remember, every great musician started just like you - with a single strum. Your dedication and practice will continue to pay off as you grow in your musical journey.

Happy strumming!